Wonderful WORLD

SECOND EDITION

WORKBOOK

Australia • Brazil • Mexico • Singapore • United Kingdom • United States

Wonderful World 5 Workbook, Second Edition

Vice President, Editorial Director:
John McHugh

Executive Editor: Siân Mavor

Commissioning Editor: Kayleigh Buller

Senior Development Editor:
Karen Haller Beer

Head of Strategic Marketing EMEA ELT:
Charlotte Ellis

Product Marketing Executive:
Ellen Setterfield

Head of Production and Design:
Celia Jones

Senior Content Project Manager:
Phillipa Davidson-Blake

Manufacturing Manager: Eyvett Davis

Art Director: Brenda Carmichael

Cover Design: Lisa Trager

Interior Design and Composition:
Lumina Datamatics, Inc.

© 2019 National Geographic Learning, a Cengage Learning Company

ALL RIGHTS RESERVED. No part of this work covered by the copyright herein may be reproduced or distributed in any form or by any means, except as permitted by U.S. copyright law, without the prior written permission of the copyright owner.

"National Geographic", "National Geographic Society" and the Yellow Border Design are registered trademarks of the National Geographic Society ® Marcas Registradas

---

For product information and technology assistance, contact us at
Cengage Learning Customer & Sales Support, cengage.com/contact

For permission to use material from this text or product,
submit all requests online at **cengage.com/permissions**
Further permissions questions can be emailed to
permissionrequest@cengage.com

Workbook: Level 5
ISBN: 978-1-4737-6065-3

National Geographic Learning
Cheriton House, North Way
Andover, Hampshire, SP10 5BE
United Kingdom

National Geographic Learning, a Cengage Learning Company, has a mission to bring the world to the classroom and the classroom to life. With our English language programs, students learn about their world by experiencing it. Through our partnerships with National Geographic and TED Talks, they develop the language and skills they need to be successful global citizens and leaders.

Locate your local office at **international.cengage.com/region**

Visit National Geographic Learning online at **ngl.cengage.com/ELT**
Visit our corporate website at **www.cengage.com**

Printed in the United Kingdom by Ashford Colour Ltd.
Print Number: 09   Print Year: 2026

Contents

	Page
Unit 0: Introduction	4
Unit 1: Fascinating Places	6
Unit 2: Science and Technology	12
Review 1: Units 1–2	18
Unit 3: Natural Wonders	20
Unit 4: Legends and Folk tales	26
Review 2: Units 3–4	32
Unit 5: Ambitions	34
Unit 6: Remarkable People	40
Review 3: Units 5–6	46
Unit 7: Body and Mind	48
Unit 8: The Arts	54
Review 4: Units 7–8	60
Unit 9: Extreme Sports	62
Unit 10: Under the Sea	68
Review 5: Units 9–10	74
Unit 11: Communication	76
Unit 12: Money	82
Review 6: Units 11–12	88
Projects: 1–12	90

0 Introduction

Adverbs of frequency

1 Match. Then complete the sentences with these words.

> sometimes   ~~always~~   never   usually   often

1 Jenny wears that shirt every day.
2 Jenny sees her grandma on Saturdays.
3 Jenny doesn't drink coffee.
4 Jenny rides her bike most days.
5 Jenny plays football four times a week.

a She _____ plays football.
b She __always__ wears it.
c She _____ sees her grandma.
d She _____ drinks it.
e She _____ rides her bike.

Possessive adjectives and pronouns

2 Circle the correct words.

1 This book is **my** / **mine**. I bought it yesterday.
2 Can I borrow **yours** / **your** pencil? I can't find mine.
3 'Which cat belongs to Samir and Ali?' 'This one is **theirs** / **their**.'
4 This house is **our** / **ours**. We love living here.
5 That bike isn't John's. **His** / **Hers** is the red one.
6 This is my sister. **Her** / **Its** name is Elsa.

Much, many, both, either, neither

3 Look at the pictures and write *T* (True) or *F* (False).

1 Neither of the children is happy. [F]
2 There aren't many balls. ☐
3 The boy can choose either of the apples. ☐
4 Both children are wearing hats. ☐
5 There isn't much sugar on the spoon. ☐

Too, enough

4 Complete the sentences with *too* or *enough*.

1. Do we have ___enough___ food for dinner?
2. Your homework is _____ difficult. I can't help you!
3. Alan isn't fast _____ to play football.
4. The dog is _____ dirty to come in the house.
5. I'm not good _____ to win the competition.

Any, every, no, some, a lot of, a few, a little

5 Circle the correct words.

Amy: I'm really hungry. Has Mum made (1) **anything** / **anywhere** for lunch?

Tim: No, she had to go (2) **somewhere** / **something** with Grandma. Shall we make a pizza?

Amy: Sure! Have we got (3) **everything** / **everybody** we need? Is there (4) **some** / **any** cheese in the fridge?

Tim: Well, there's (5) **a lot of** / **a little**, but I don't think there's enough for a pizza. There are (6) **a few** / **a little** olives and there's (7) **some** / **much** tomato sauce.

Amy: Yuck. I don't like olives. What about mushrooms? I love mushrooms on a pizza.

Tim: Sorry, there are (8) **a little** / **no** mushrooms. I ate them all for breakfast.

Amy: I know … where's the phone?

Tim: Why? What are you going to do?

Amy: Hello. Dino's Pizzas? I want to order a big pizza with tomato sauce, cheese and mushrooms, please!

Question tags

6 Complete the sentences with question tags.

1. You don't know Alex, ___do you___?
2. The fridge isn't empty, _____?
3. The boys played football yesterday, _____?
4. Carla has left, _____?
5. Jake lives near here, _____?
6. Mum didn't give you a message, _____?

Adverbs of manner

7 Complete the sentences with adverbs of manner.

1. Children, I want you to play ___nicely___ (nice) together.
2. You've done very _____ (good) this term, Cindy.
3. The cat climbed _____ (high) up into the tree and wouldn't come down.
4. I think Simon will _____ (easy) pass the exam.
5. Don't drive so _____ (fast)! It's dangerous!
6. Hani always arrives _____ (late) for class.
7. Please wash the vase _____ (careful).
8. Come here _____ (quick)! There's a fox in the garden!

1 Fascinating Places

Lesson 1

1 Complete the sentences with these words.

fascinating   ~~border~~   monument   prehistoric   ruins

1 We show our passports when we cross the _____border_____.
2 There is a _____ of our national hero in the park.
3 I love visiting old _____ of castles.
4 Peru is such a _____ country!
5 There is a _____ fort made from enormous stones.

2 Match.

1 sculpture [e]   3 palace [ ]   5 fountain [ ]
2 market   [ ]   4 bridge [ ]

a

c

e

b

d

3 Circle the odd one out.

1 fascinating	exciting	(ugly)
2 modern	wide	high
3 ancient	massive	prehistoric
4 town	palace	house
5 monument	sculpture	market
6 close	fountain	bridge

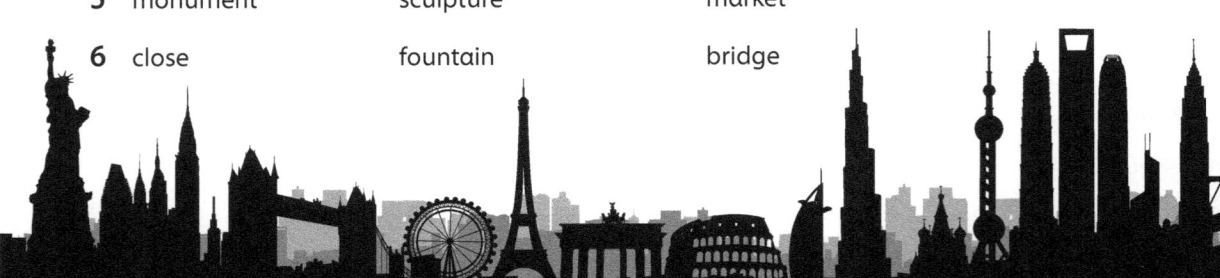

6 UNIT 1

4 Complete the sentences with the present simple or the present continuous of these verbs.

cross   leave   not be   not drive   open   ~~speak~~   walk   write

1 My friend is from France and she ___speaks___ English and French.
2 Hold my hand, Tommy. We _____ the road now.
3 In this photo, we _____ round the gardens at Hampton Court Palace.
4 The Heritage Museum _____ at 9 o'clock every morning.
5 We _____ to London. It's too far.
6 My mum always _____ a travel diary when we go on holiday.
7 _____ Tom _____ for London next week?
8 The weather in Scotland _____ very good. It often rains.

5 Write questions and short answers with the present simple or the present continuous.

1 they / stay near here ✓
   Are they staying near here?
   Yes, they are.

2 your parents / enjoy travelling ✓
   _____
   _____

3 the visitors / go to Cusco tomorrow ✗
   _____
   _____

4 you / sell maps in this shop ✓
   _____
   _____

5 Jim / know the way to Machu Picchu ✗
   _____
   _____

6 Complete the dialogue with the present simple or the present continuous of the verbs in brackets.

Jane: (1) ___Do you always come___ (you / always / come) to Wales on holiday?

Bob: Yes, we (2) _____ (love) it here.

Jane: (3) _____ (you / stay) at the campsite this week?

Bob: Yes, we are. Then next week we (4) _____ (drive) to Prestatyn in our camper van.

Jane: Prestatyn? (5) _____ (they / speak) Welsh in Prestatyn?

Bob: Yes, they do, but they (6) _____ (speak) English too. We (7) _____ (visit) an old Roman site near there on Wednesday. It (8) _____ (not be) very famous, but I think it's quite interesting.

Jane: I hope you have a good time there. Enjoy yourselves!

7

Lesson 2

1 Match.

1 river   c
2 walking boots
3 shade
4 map
5 guidebook
6 rafting

2 Circle the correct words.

1 These ruins have been here for the **past** / **most** 300 years.
2 At one **bridge** / **point** the lake is 1,000 metres deep.
3 This gorge is really **beautiful** / **narrow**. Cars can't drive down it.
4 This water is too **easy** / **rocky** for rafting.
5 It's easy to cycle on a **cold** / **flat** road.
6 I don't like rafting in **powerful** / **big** water. It's scary!
7 We can walk through the water where it's **shallow** / **deep**.
8 This **sculpture** / **gorge** has fascinating plants in it.

3 Complete the sentences with these words.

| in | ~~wide~~ | down | back | steep | on | in | suggests |

1 This river is too ____wide____ to swim across.
2 You need good walking boots for climbing _____ hills.
3 Let's get _____ the bus. It's faster than walking.
4 Our research _____ that people are living longer.
5 When are you coming _____ from your holidays?
6 First, we have to check _____ at the hotel.
7 Jerry's motorbike sometimes breaks _____ on the road.
8 Get _____ the car, everybody. It's time to go home.

8 UNIT 1

4 Complete the sentences with the present simple or the present continuous of these verbs.

> belong   drive   know   not understand   ~~smell~~   walk

1 These wild flowers near the path _____smell_____ lovely.

2 They _____ to France in their car.

3 I _____ this map. It's really difficult to read.

4 These walking boots _____ to Jenny.

5 The hikers _____ through the gorge tomorrow.

6 _____ you _____ who built Machu Picchu?

5 Complete the email with the present simple or the present continuous of the verbs in brackets.

Hi Mary,

Guess what? I (1) ___am staying___ (stay) on a horse ranch in Arizona for the summer! It (2) _____ (belong) to my Aunt Polly. It's fantastic! Aunt Polly (3) _____ (own) eight horses and two ponies. My favourite is a big brown horse called Nutmeg – I (4) _____ (love) her. You can see her in the photo I (5) _____ (send) you with this email. She (6) _____ (be) beautiful and she (7) _____ (like) chocolate! (8) _____ (you / have) a good time in Jordan? Send me an email and tell me all about it.

Love from Lisa

6 Circle the correct words.

1 I **am seeing** / **see** my archaeology teacher at ten o'clock.

2 I **am thinking** / **think** of going rafting on the Colorado River.

3 This path looks dangerous. **Are you seeing** / **Do you see** what I mean?

4 I **am not thinking** / **don't think** the bus is coming. Let's go home.

5 I **am thinking** / **think** the ancient monuments in Peru are fascinating.

Lesson 3

1 Write the missing letters.

1 These are people who visit a place. t o u r i s t s
2 This season comes before summer. s _ _ _ _ _
3 This is a large area of water. l _ _ _
4 Trains use this. r _ _ _ _ _ _
5 This is someone aged between 13 and 19. t _ _ _ _ _ _ _
6 This is a sandy area near the sea. b _ _ _ _

2 Complete the sentences with *who*, *whose*, *which*, *where* or *when* and these phrases.

> is really famous   sister visited India   ~~studies old places and things~~
> the Romans built Hadrian's Wall   the visitors got lost

1 An archaeologist is a person **who studies old places and things**.
2 122 CE is the year _____.
3 The Grand Canyon, _____, is in Arizona.
4 Paul, _____, wants to travel there too.
5 The monument, _____, is in the museum.

3 Match.

SAY IT LIKE THIS!

1 When's your birthday?   a Once a year.
2 What are you doing at the moment?   b It's at five o'clock.
3 How often do you go on holiday?   c No, never.
4 Are you ever late for school?   d On May 1st.
5 What time is your piano lesson?   e No, I usually cycle.
6 Do you walk to school?   f I'm reading a book about India.

4 Complete the description of Peter's home town with these words and phrases.

> it is   there are   there is   they are
> when   where   ~~which~~   who

I live in a market town (1) ___which___ is called Ludlow. (2) _____ near the border between Wales and England. The best time to visit Ludlow is in the summer (3) _____ the Ludlow Festival takes place.

(4) _____ a fascinating old castle (5) _____ visitors can learn about life in the past and watch Shakespeare plays. The actors (6) _____ take part in the plays are usually very famous.

You can also take a trip by boat along the river, or walk around the riverside gardens. (7) _____ full of flowers in summer. (8) _____ also great restaurants, shops and cafés.

Remember!

We use **There is / are** to talk about something that exists or happens that we mention for the first time.

We use **It is** and **They are** to refer to something that has already been mentioned or is being talked about now.

There is a pathway over the gorge. **It is** made of glass.
There are four tourists in the café. **They are** from Japan.

5 Write a description of your village or town. Include relative clauses, *There is*, *There are*, *It is* and *They are*. Use this plan to help you.

> **Paragraph 1** – Give the name of your town or village and say where it is situated.
>
> **Paragraph 2** – Talk about what you can see and do there.
>
> **Paragraph 3** – Talk about other activities or places of interest.

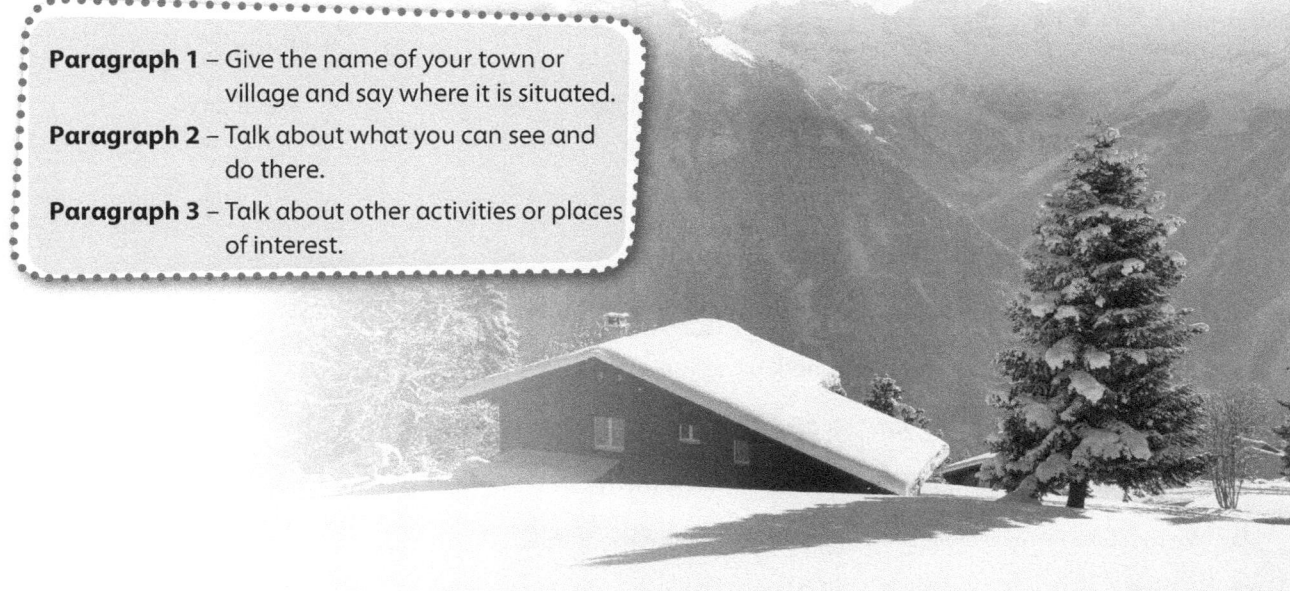

2 Science and Technology

Lesson 1

1 Complete the sentences with these words.

| absorb | create | smooth | glow | ~~power~~ | rays |

1 He built a house which uses solar ___power___ for all its energy.
2 These panels _____ light from the sun.
3 The stars _____ in the sky at night.
4 Artists _____ things like pictures and sculptures.
5 The sun's _____ are very bright and hot.
6 _____ paths can become too slippery for cyclists.

2 Match.

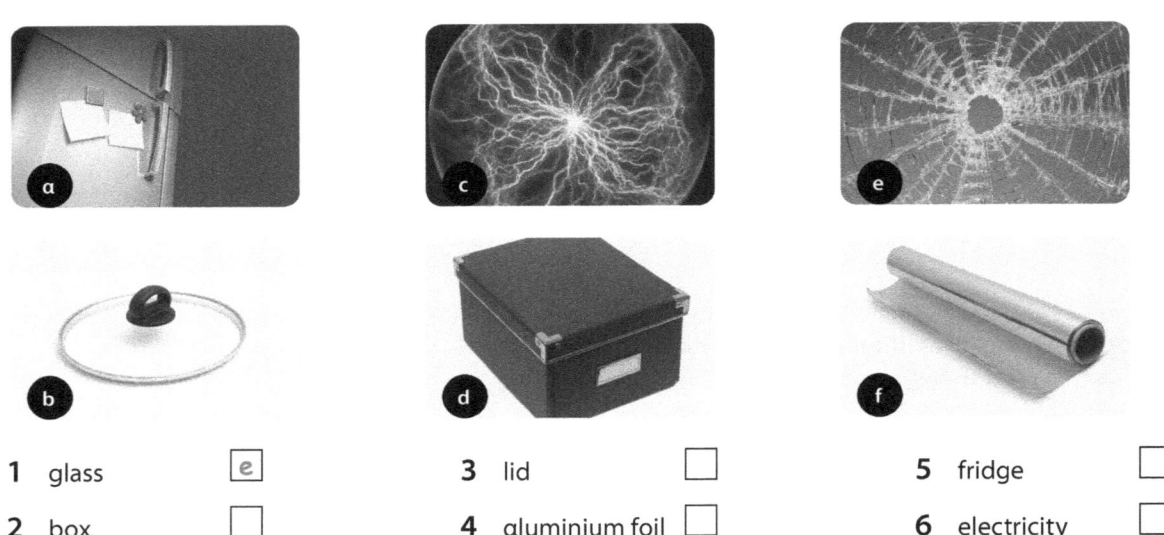

1 glass   e
2 box   ☐
3 lid   ☐
4 aluminium foil ☐
5 fridge   ☐
6 electricity ☐

3 Circle the correct words.

1 Can you **do** / **make** me a favour, please?
2 Oh dear! I've **done** / **made** a mistake in my science project.
3 We are **doing** / **making** an experiment using the solar panels.
4 Did you **do** / **make** the homework about the sun and the planets?
5 Ssh! Don't **do** / **make** a sound or the birds will fly away!
6 We must **do** / **make** a decision about where to put the fridge.
7 Katy **did** / **made** some research on the Internet for her physics project.
8 The children are **doing** / **making** a big effort to understand the instructions.

4 Choose the correct answers.

1 Andy _____ a picture of his new invention last week.
   a) drew
   b) was drawing
   c) draw

2 _____ an experiment when I phoned you?
   a) You were doing
   b) Did you do
   c) Were you doing

3 We were looking at the robot and the teacher _____ .
   a) talked
   b) was talking
   c) talks

4 _____ your science homework at six o'clock last night?
   a) You did
   b) Did you
   c) Were you doing

5 I _____ to my physics class yesterday because I was ill.
   a) didn't go
   b) wasn't going
   c) not going

6 His dad was playing a game while his mum _____ a letter.
   a) is writing
   b) writing
   c) was writing

5 Complete the article with the past simple or the past continuous of the verbs in brackets.

LIFE ON MARS?

The Phoenix Mars Lander (1) ___took off___ (take off) on 4th August 2007 and after a seven-month journey it (2) _____ (land) on Mars in May 2008. A short time later, it (3) _____ (make) an amazing discovery.

While the 'arm' of the Lander (4) _____ (dig) in the soil, something shiny (5) _____ (appear). The camera on the arm (6) _____ (allow) scientists on earth to see this, and they (7) _____ (be) very excited about the discovery. As science expert Joseph Rogers explains: 'The scientists had found what they (8) _____ (look) for – ice! Ice means water, and water means that one day humans might be able to live on the red planet.'

6 Look at the pictures of Wendy ten years ago and now. Make sentences with *used to*.

1 Wendy / wear / glasses
   Wendy used to wear glasses.

2 Wendy / have / long hair
   _____

3 Wendy / have / a car
   _____

4 Wendy / go to school / on roller skates
   _____

5 Wendy / wear / expensive clothes
   _____

6 Wendy / have / a mobile phone
   _____

Lesson 2

1 Match.

1 outer space   b
2 planet
3 telescope
4 solar system
5 galaxy
6 spacecraft

2 Circle the correct words.

1 You need to concentrate **in** / **on** your science project.
2 The astronauts have to deal **with** / **for** some technical problems before they return to Earth.
3 The president congratulated the astronomers **on** / **in** their new discovery.
4 The astronauts are depending **on** / **for** the spaceship's computer to bring them safely home.
5 Scientists have spent years searching **in** / **for** new planets in space.
6 The astronaut succeeded **in** / **with** fixing the spaceship.

3 Complete the sentences with these words.

> discovered   ~~exists~~   microscopic   investigate   orbits   supported   surface   universe

1 Scientists want to know if life ____exists____ on other planets.
2 Yesterday, we _____ a duck in our bathroom!
3 Be careful! The _____ of the road is very icy this morning.
4 For my geography project, I'm going to _____ volcanoes.
5 The _____ is huge.
6 There are _____ insects living on this leaf.
7 Has the planet Mars ever _____ life?
8 The planet Earth _____ the sun once every year.

14 UNIT 2

4 Complete the sentences with the past simple or the present perfect simple of the verbs in brackets.

1. I __watched__ (watch) a fantastic documentary about the International Space Station last night.
2. Kerry _____ (finish) her project about space travel. It's on her desk.
3. A total of 12 astronauts _____ (walk) on the Moon.
4. I _____ (not know) that scientists _____ (find) ice on Mars last month!
5. Seven astronauts _____ (die) in the space shuttle Challenger in 1986.
6. _____ you _____ (ever / hear) of Laika, the first dog in space?
7. The astronauts _____ (succeed) in landing on the Moon.
8. He _____ (teach) physics at the university for ten years before he moved to Scotland.

5 Circle the correct words.

Astronauts must train before they go into space. Last year, six 'astronauts' (1) **have spent / (spent)** 105 days shut inside a model spaceship. During that time they (2) **had to / have had to** work and live as if they (3) **were / have been** on a real spaceship travelling to Mars.

When 'astronaut' Oliver Knickel (4) **has stepped / stepped** out of the 'spaceship' after three months he said, 'We (5) **have just completed / just completed** our mission. We hope that the information we (6) **have collected / collected** since the start of our journey will help the real mission to Mars.'

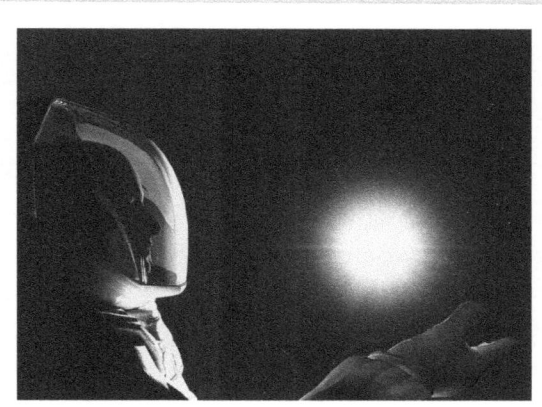

6 Complete the sentences with these words.

ago   already   ever   for   last night   never   since   yet

1. I've __already__ read that book about Neil Armstrong. It was great!
2. The spaceship left Earth two months _____ .
3. Tom has _____ been to the Science Museum, but he really wants to go.
4. We saw the International Space Station in the sky _____ .
5. The shuttle has orbited the Earth _____ 16 days.
6. She has wanted to become an astronaut _____ she was young.
7. I haven't finished my science homework _____ .
8. Have you _____ seen Mars in the sky?

Lesson 3

1 Complete the crossword puzzle.

Down

1 This is the scientific knowledge used to design machines.
2 This is another word for someone who helps.
4 We wear these on our feet when we want to exercise.

Across

3 There's lots of this in the summer.
5 This is a cool invention.
6 This is another word for *way*.

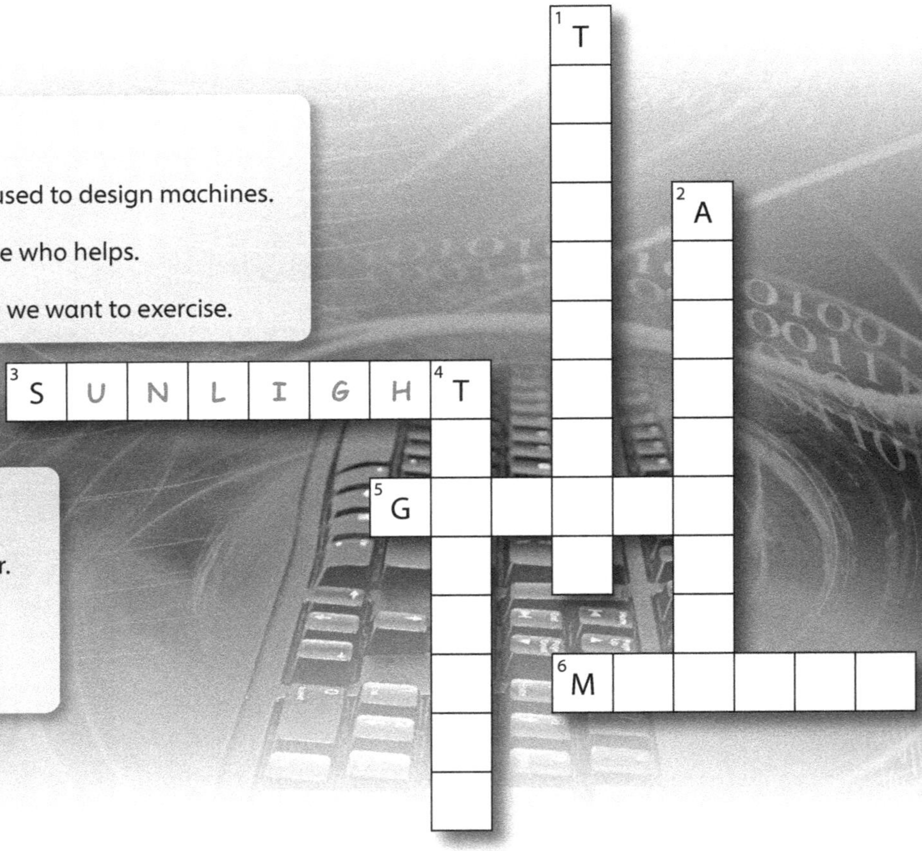

Crossword:
- 1 Down: T...
- 2 Down: A...
- 3 Across: SUNLIGHT
- 4 Down: T...
- 5 Across: G...
- 6 Across: M...

2 Match.

SAY IT LIKE THIS!

1 He spoke so quickly
2 We had such
3 The telephone is such
4 She was so tired
5 Their everyday life is so busy
6 We did such an exciting experiment

a in our science lesson today.
b that she went to bed.
c a useful invention.
d that I didn't understand him.
e an amazing laptop before you broke it.
f because they work and have children.

3 Work with a partner to make sentences. Use these prompts to talk about the people. Use *so* and *such*.

Helen Dion
a good singer
beautiful
a talented songwriter

My best friend
clever
a good listener
funny

The Smith Brothers
good clothes
great songs
popular

16 UNIT 2

4 Read the email below and put the paragraphs in the correct order.

Hi Gemma,

[4] Finally, it's got lots of brilliant games. There are so many that I haven't played all of them yet!

[ ] My new phone is great for lots of reasons. First of all, it's a fantastic colour – it's red. It's so cool! It also comes in orange and black, but red is my favourite colour.

[ ] How are you? It was my birthday yesterday and I got lots of amazing presents. I'm so excited because my parents bought me a new mobile phone. I used to have a phone, but it was such an old model that it didn't even take photos!

[ ] Secondly, you can save songs from the Internet on the phone. I've already got 100 songs on mine! In addition, it's got a digital camera. It also has a video camera. You can add words and music to your photos or videos and send them to your friends!

Write soon with your news!
Helen

Remember!

We use these words and phrases to put ideas in order in a letter or email.
Firstly / First of all / To start with
Secondly / In addition
Finally
We use **also** and **too** to add new points.
My mobile phone takes photos. It takes videos **too**.
My mobile phone takes photos. It **also** takes videos.

5 Write an email to a friend about a new telescope. Include linking words. Use this plan to help you.

Begin like this:
Hi (your friend's name),

Paragraph 1
Ask how your friend is. Tell your friend why somebody gave you a new telescope.

Paragraph 2
Talk about the colour/shape/size of your telescope and why you like it.

Paragraph 3
Talk about the best/most exciting things about your telescope.

Paragraph 4
Talk about what you can and can't see with your telescope.

Finish like this:
Write soon with your news!
(your name)

Review 1 — Units 1–2

1 Read the text about the Eiffel Tower.

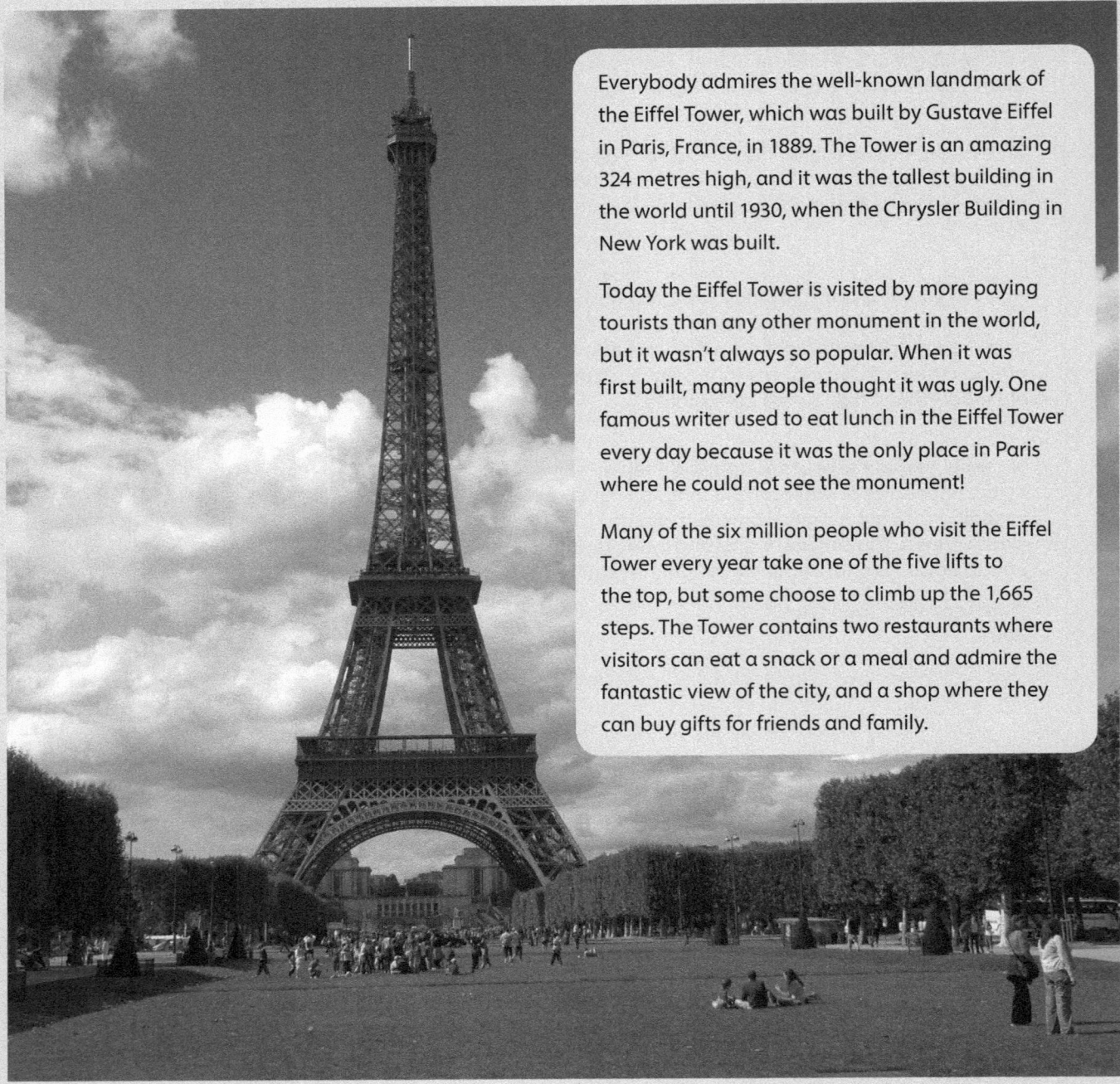

Everybody admires the well-known landmark of the Eiffel Tower, which was built by Gustave Eiffel in Paris, France, in 1889. The Tower is an amazing 324 metres high, and it was the tallest building in the world until 1930, when the Chrysler Building in New York was built.

Today the Eiffel Tower is visited by more paying tourists than any other monument in the world, but it wasn't always so popular. When it was first built, many people thought it was ugly. One famous writer used to eat lunch in the Eiffel Tower every day because it was the only place in Paris where he could not see the monument!

Many of the six million people who visit the Eiffel Tower every year take one of the five lifts to the top, but some choose to climb up the 1,665 steps. The Tower contains two restaurants where visitors can eat a snack or a meal and admire the fantastic view of the city, and a shop where they can buy gifts for friends and family.

2 Write *R* (Right), *W* (Wrong) or *DS* (Doesn't Say).

1. The Eiffel Tower is now the tallest building in France. — DS
2. The Chrysler Building is in New York.
3. The Eiffel Tower was finished in 1930.
4. In 1889, lots of people didn't like the Tower.
5. Six million people take the lifts to the top of the Tower every year.
6. The food in the restaurants is delicious.

3 Choose the correct answers.

1 The tourists ___ lost in the woods.
   a found
   b went
   c (got)

2 We'll arrive at the ___ in three hours.
   a rafting
   b border
   c point

3 The river runs through a beautiful ___ .
   a ruin
   b gorge
   c sculpture

4 Many modern ___ make life a lot easier.
   a messages
   b gadgets
   c boots

5 We're doing an ___ in our chemistry lesson today.
   a experiment
   b invention
   c observatory

6 I want to congratulate you ___ winning the competition!
   a in
   b on
   c at

7 The path up to the palace is very ___ .
   a powerful
   b fascinating
   c steep

8 The river is too wide and ___ to swim in.
   a shallow
   b flat
   c smooth

9 We discovered some ___ life forms in the water.
   a microscopic
   b orbiting
   c surface

10 ___ is created by the sun's rays.
   a A telescope
   b Shade
   c Solar power

11 I was asleep when the plane ___ .
   a went away
   b took off
   c got on

12 How are we going to ___ with this problem?
   a depend
   b succeed
   c deal

4 Choose the correct answers.

1 We ___ to London tomorrow.
   a (are driving)
   b have driven
   c were driving

2 ___ visiting museums when you're on holiday?
   a Are you enjoying
   b Do you enjoy
   c You do enjoy

3 ___ in developing his scientific ideas last year?
   a Did he succeed
   b Was he succeeding
   c He did succeed

4 We ___ an experiment when the electricity went off.
   a was doing
   b did
   c were doing

5 This flower ___ lovely.
   a smells
   b is smelling
   c smell

6 The man ___ car was parked here has driven away.
   a which
   b whose
   c who's

7 ___ the prehistoric circle next week?
   a Is your class visiting
   b Does your class visit
   c Did your class visit

8 ___ that book about the scientist yet?
   a Did you finish
   b Have you finished
   c Were you finishing

9 ___ what I'm saying about the experiment?
   a Are you seeing
   b Do you see
   c Have you seen

10 We were hiking up a mountain when we ___ our way.
   a have lost
   b were losing
   c lost

11 They were working on the cycle path ___ yesterday.
   a for the day
   b all day
   c long day

12 Jim has ___ to visit the Space Museum.
   a gone
   b went
   c done

3 Natural Wonders

Lesson 1

1 Write the missing letters.

1. This is when there is lots of water everywhere.   f <u>l o o d</u>
2. This is a huge wave.   t _ _ _ _ _ _
3. When there is no rain for a long time, this happens.   d _ _ _ _ _ _
4. Hot rocks and lava come out of this.   v _ _ _ _ _ _
5. This is a big fire that's hard to put out.   w _ _ _ _ _ _ _
6. A terrible storm like this causes lots of damage.   h _ _ _ _ _ _ _

2 Circle the odd one out.

1. flood — (cause) — drought
2. equipment — burn — spread
3. cause — create — prevent
4. flood — tsunami — power
5. burn — put out — wildfire
6. move — spread — stop

3 Complete the sentences with these words.

| caused | burn | damaged | ~~wildfire~~ | prevent | emergency |

1. The ____wildfire____ is spreading quickly and the firefighters can't stop it.
2. You can always call me in an _____.
3. The hurricane has _____ the school and all the houses.
4. It's easier to _____ a fire than to put it out.
5. Tsunamis are often _____ by earthquakes.
6. You should take the pizza out of the oven or it will _____.

4 Choose the correct answers.

1 We _____ on the island for two weeks.
 a have been staying
 b stay
 c been staying

2 _____ have you been working at the information centre?
 a What
 b How long
 c What time

3 _____ watching the news? There was a tsunami in India.
 a You have been
 b Have you been
 c You haven't been to

4 The wind _____ all day long today.
 a blows
 b is blowing
 c has been blowing

5 Dad has been cycling to work _____ May.
 a for
 b since
 c all

5 Write questions and answers with the present perfect continuous and the words in brackets.

1 how long / you study / tropical fish (two months)
 How long have you been studying tropical fish?
 I've been studying tropical fish for two months.

2 the situation / on the island / improve (no)
 _____
 _____

3 the students / plant / trees (yes)
 _____
 _____

4 how long / Paolo / work / as a volunteer (July)
 _____
 _____

5 you / walk / in the mountains / all day (yes)
 _____
 _____

6 Complete the email with the present perfect continuous of the verbs in brackets.

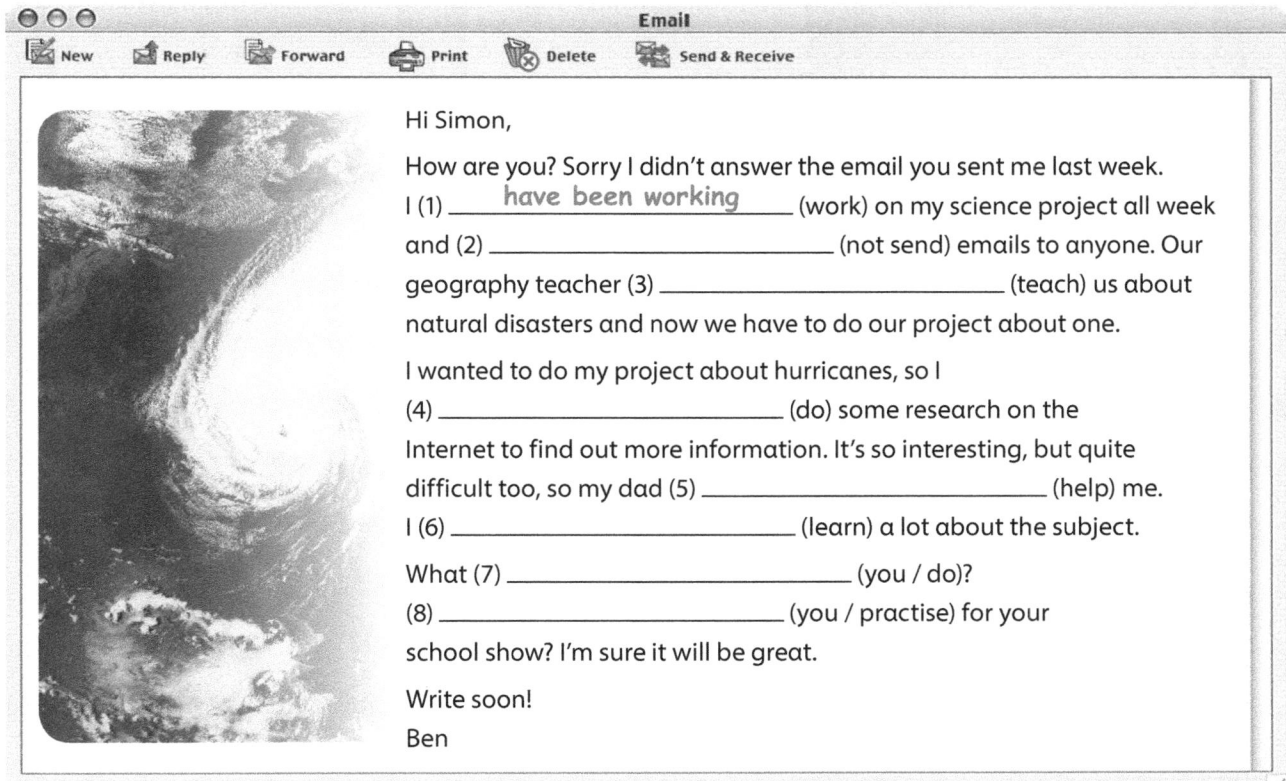

Hi Simon,

How are you? Sorry I didn't answer the email you sent me last week. I (1) _have been working_ (work) on my science project all week and (2) _____ (not send) emails to anyone. Our geography teacher (3) _____ (teach) us about natural disasters and now we have to do our project about one.

I wanted to do my project about hurricanes, so I (4) _____ (do) some research on the Internet to find out more information. It's so interesting, but quite difficult too, so my dad (5) _____ (help) me. I (6) _____ (learn) a lot about the subject.

What (7) _____ (you / do)?
(8) _____ (you / practise) for your school show? I'm sure it will be great.

Write soon!
Ben

Lesson 2

1 Circle the correct words.

1 The platypus is an unusual **mammal** / **reptile** because it lays eggs.
2 The king vulture has a colourful **horn** / **appearance**.
3 Lizards, snakes and frogs are all **beaks** / **reptiles**.
4 Short-horned lizards use their eyes to trick **predators** / **species**.
5 All animals need to be good at **defending** / **stopping** themselves.
6 The duck-billed platypus is a fascinating **bird** / **species**.

2 Label the pictures with these words.

bill   ~~beak~~   claws   fur   horns   scales

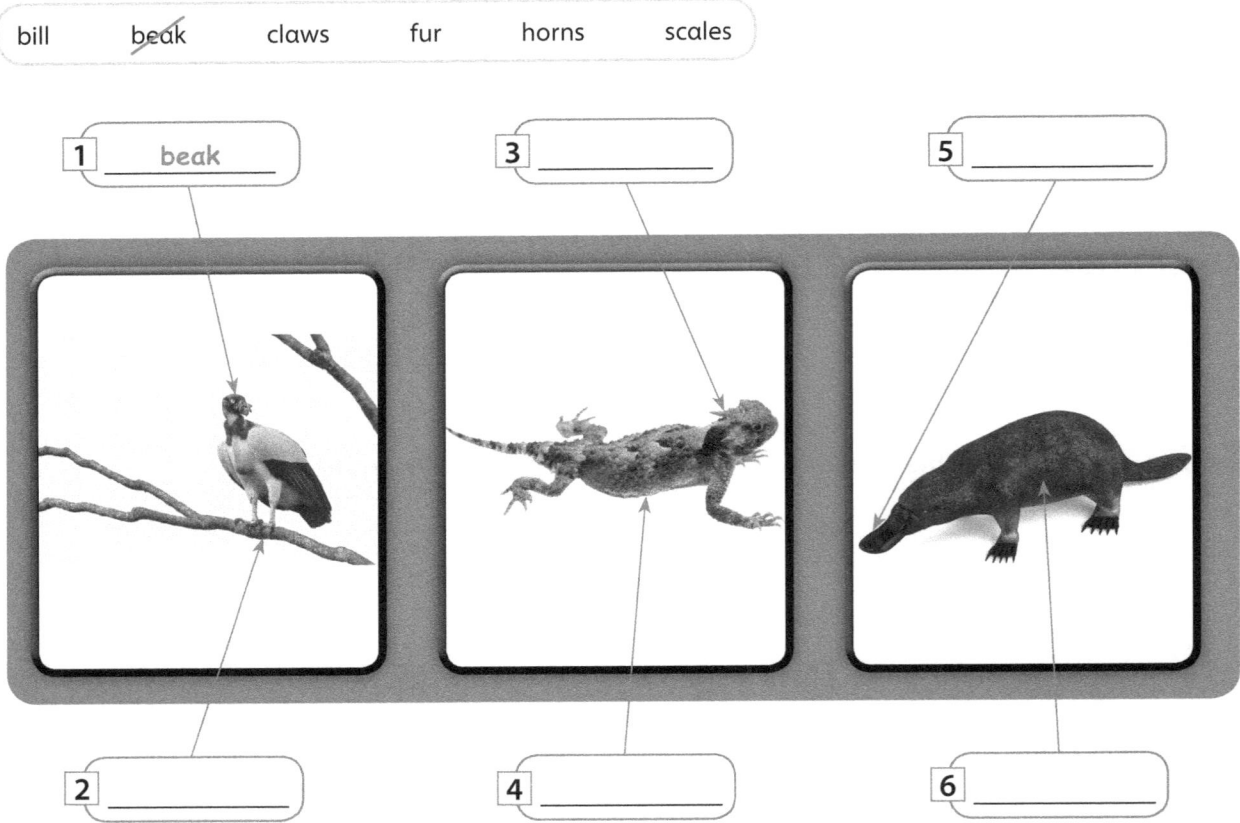

1 beak
2 ____
3 ____
4 ____
5 ____
6 ____

3 Match.

1 People must cut
2 Some tropical fish are dying
3 Are scientists looking
4 What will we do when the world runs
5 Petrol companies must answer
6 It's important that we get

a into ways of preventing air pollution?
b for the damage they are doing to the environment.
c out of oil?
d down on the amount of energy they use.
e our message across.
f out because of pollution in the sea.

22 UNIT 3

4 Complete the sentences with the present perfect simple or the present perfect continuous of the verbs in brackets.

1 I _____'ve read_____ (read) this article about solar power three times, but I still don't understand it.
2 Tom _____ (not wash) his car all morning. He has been reading.
3 _____ (you / see) the film *Finding Nemo* about a clown fish?
4 We _____ (just / finish) our science exam. It was really difficult!
5 Amani _____ (not sleep) well since the earthquake.
6 Oh no! We _____ (run) out of paper. I can't print out my project.
7 We _____ (learn) about plankton in our biology class this week.
8 How many times _____ (you / be) to the Natural History Museum?

5 Circle the correct words.

1 **Have you watered** / **Have you been watering** the flowers today?
2 **How many times** / **How many photos** of the animals have you taken?
3 I **have watched** / **have been watching** this brilliant programme about lizards. Why don't you come and watch it with me?
4 Polly **has read** / **has been reading** that book four times!
5 Carl **has been planting** / **has planted** new trees on Cortuga for years.
6 I **have been finding** / **have found** some fossils in my garden.

6 Complete the dialogue with the present perfect simple or the present perfect continuous of the verbs in brackets.

Anna: Hi Gina. What (1) __have you been doing__ (you / do) lately?

Gina: I (2) _____ (look) on the Internet and I (3) _____ (find) this website about an amazing show in London. It's called *Walking with Dinosaurs*. Scientists and inventors (4) _____ (create) 15 life-size dinosaurs. I (5) _____ (read) about it all morning. It's brilliant.

Anna: Do you mean they (6) _____ (made) dinosaurs that look real?

Gina: Yes, they actually walk around and roar! The scientists (7) _____ (build) models of dinosaurs which use computer technology. It says on the website that they (8) _____ (work) on this project for years.

Anna: That sounds fantastic.

Lesson 3

1 Circle the correct words.

1 We're going to the southern **coast** / **park** of Iceland next week.
2 The sea is very **melted** / **clear** today.
3 It was a difficult journey, but it was **good** / **worth** it.
4 The Earth's **ocean** / **atmosphere** is full of gases.
5 The stars **arrive** / **appear** in the sky every night.
6 Your torch is **shining** / **making** in my eyes!

2 Complete the article with the correct comparative or superlative structure of the adjectives / adverbs in brackets.

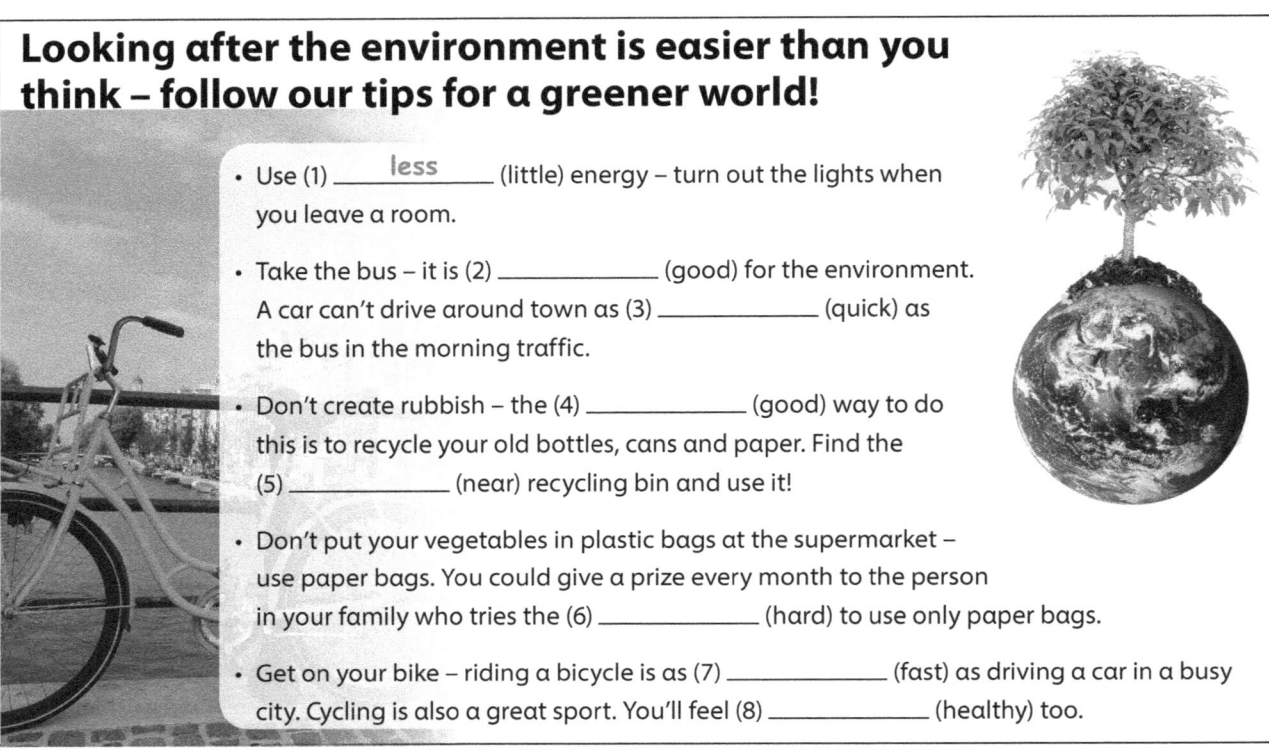

Looking after the environment is easier than you think – follow our tips for a greener world!

- Use (1) _____less_____ (little) energy – turn out the lights when you leave a room.

- Take the bus – it is (2) _____ (good) for the environment. A car can't drive around town as (3) _____ (quick) as the bus in the morning traffic.

- Don't create rubbish – the (4) _____ (good) way to do this is to recycle your old bottles, cans and paper. Find the (5) _____ (near) recycling bin and use it!

- Don't put your vegetables in plastic bags at the supermarket – use paper bags. You could give a prize every month to the person in your family who tries the (6) _____ (hard) to use only paper bags.

- Get on your bike – riding a bicycle is as (7) _____ (fast) as driving a car in a busy city. Cycling is also a great sport. You'll feel (8) _____ (healthy) too.

3 Complete the sentences with *it's worth*, or *it isn't worth* and the verbs in brackets.

SAY IT LIKE THIS!

1 It's one o'clock. The next bus comes at three o'clock. (wait)
   It isn't worth waiting because the next bus doesn't come until three o'clock.

2 He doesn't like chocolate ice cream. (buy)
   _____

3 Study now. The exams are next week. (study)
   _____

4 Why don't you keep those old books? They cost a lot of money. (keep)
   _____

24 UNIT 3

4 Read the letter to a newspaper and circle the correct words.

Dear Sir/Madam,

Yesterday there was an article in your newspaper about cars and the environment. I (1) **agree** / disagree that cars create pollution and are one of the reasons that our climate is changing. We should stop using them!

Today every family has one, or even two, cars. Most people drive everywhere – to the shops, to work and to school. People know that cars are harmful to the environment, but they still use them all the time. In my (2) **belief** / **opinion**, we should try to use cars less and cycle or walk more.

If your work or your school is close to your home, you can walk or cycle there. Walking and cycling don't cause air pollution, and you will become fitter and healthier if you cycle to school every day! It (3) **is** / **isn't** always true that cars are faster than bicycles. Sometimes a bicycle is much faster than a car on busy town roads.

If people leave their cars at home and walk or cycle to nearby places, then I (4) **agree** / **believe** that we will be able to reduce air pollution and improve our fitness.

Yours faithfully,
Drew Parker

Remember!

You can use these words and phrases to give your opinion about something when you are writing a formal email or letter.
I (really) think / believe …
In my opinion / view …
It is / isn't true that …
I agree / disagree that …

5 Write a letter to your school newspaper giving your opinion about how your school can do more to help the environment. Use this plan to help you.

Begin like this:
Dear Sir / Madam,

Paragraph 1
Mention an article in the school newspaper that you have read about how each person can help the environment. Say if you agree or disagree.

Paragraph 2
Talk about one thing pupils can do. Say how this could be done and what the advantages are.

Paragraph 3
Talk about another thing pupils and teachers can do. Say how this could be done and what the advantages are.

Paragraph 4
Give a summary of how schools should encourage pupils to get involved in environmental projects.

End like this:
Yours faithfully,
(your name)

4 Legends and Folk tales

Lesson 1

1 Complete the crossword puzzle.

Across

1. Do lots of boats d__isappear__ in bad weather?
6. There's a t_____ that The Bermuda Triangle is dangerous.
7. We have e_____ that too many sweets are bad for you.

Down

2. There was a s_____ at the bottom of the sea.
3. The legend of the Bermuda Triangle isn't a m_____ any more.
4. Don't enter that old building! It's a danger z_____.
5. Yesterday, there was a car c_____ in our road.

```
¹D  I  ²S  A  P  P  E  A  R
       ³M       ⁴Z
                            ⁵C
        ⁶T
⁷E
```

2 Complete the sentences using *dis-, im-, ir-, -less,* or *un-*.

1. You've lost the thread! You're very care___less___!
2. Don't be so _____patient! We've only been waiting five minutes.
3. I believe he is _____honest because he lied about visiting Stonehenge.
4. What is that _____pleasant smell?
5. It's very _____responsible to use your mobile phone while driving.
6. Ariadne was not _____kind to Theseus; she had helped him escape.

3 Complete the sentences with these words.

| ~~careful~~   honest   foolish   pleasant   responsible   wise |

1. Be ___careful___ when you cycle to town.
2. I'm _____ for my dog in the park.
3. Going for a picnic in the rain was _____.
4. Samantha is a very _____ person. She never lies.
5. We had a very _____ evening in the restaurant. The food was great!
6. It's not _____ to go sailing in a hurricane.

26 UNIT 4

4 Complete the sentences with the past perfect simple of the verbs in brackets.

1. Mum ___hadn't locked___ (not lock) the door before she went to work. She had forgotten.
2. By the time Wendy got to the bus stop, the bus _____ (already / leave).
3. Jenny _____ (never / see) a zebra before.
4. By ten o'clock the children _____ (not go) to sleep. They were still watching the DVD.
5. Tom _____ (already / eat) his dinner when Pam got home.
6. Carol went to bed after she _____ (clean) her room.

5 Choose the correct answers.

1. By Monday morning I _____ my project on legends.
   a. have finished
   b. finish
   c. had finished ✓

2. Peter had visited Stonehenge and Hampton Court Palace _____ he went back to London.
   a. by
   b. before
   c. after

3. They _____ a pleasant meal before they went to the museum.
   a. had eaten
   b. have eaten
   c. eaten

4. _____ June 15th he had finished all of his exams.
   a. By
   b. Until
   c. Already

5. I _____ of Knossos before I read this book about Crete.
   a. didn't hear
   b. never heard
   c. had never heard

6. Katy _____ ancient Greek at school, so she knew all the Greek myths.
   a. have studied
   b. had studied
   c. study

6 Complete the sentences with the correct form of the past perfect simple of these verbs.

escape   ~~not see~~   not turn   sail   give

1. We ___had not seen___ the pyramids before we went to Egypt.
2. I _____ my brother the book before he went away to university.
3. By the time we remembered to close the door, our dog _____ .
4. We _____ all the way home before nightfall.
5. The cake burned because we _____ the oven off in time.

27

Lesson 2

1 Circle the correct words.

1 Amelia Earhart was **heading** / **flying** for the island of Howland when she disappeared.

2 The plane had taken **off** / **on** from New Guinea, but it never arrived.

3 The world **record** / **song** for flying across the Atlantic had been broken by Earhart.

4 It's important that planes have enough **food** / **fuel** for their journeys.

5 Some people think that Earhart **landed** / **took** on another island.

6 No one knows what happened to Earhart, so she will always be a **story** / **legend**.

2 Complete the sentences with these phrases.

| of | to | at | about | for | in | of | for |

1 I don't think Annie is capable ___of___ flying a plane.

2 Mark has always been really good _____ solving mysteries.

3 The pilot is responsible _____ all the passengers.

4 Is Jerry interested _____ the story about the Mary Celeste?

5 Amelia wasn't worried _____ losing her way.

6 Are you afraid _____ the dark?

7 Do you think this story is suitable _____ a child?

8 Mary was generous _____ Ken and helped him with the project.

3 Choose the correct answers.

1 Did you get a _____ to visit the Amelia Earhart museum?
   a chance
   b course
   c choice

2 I _____ a surprise when I found my cousins from India at the door.
   a took
   b got
   c found

3 I wrote Anna a message but I never got a _____ .
   a day
   b legend
   c reply

4 Graham really wants to _____ a job as a pilot. He loves flying.
   a make
   b get
   c turn

5 Dinner's ready and you're not here! When are you getting _____ ?
   a home
   b a house
   c food

6 I got the _____ that Jill worked in an office. She is actually a student.
   a surprise
   b impression
   c experience

4 Complete the sentences using the past simple or the past perfect simple.

1 Emily cried. She cut her finger.
   Emily ____cried____ because she ____had cut____ her finger.

2 Danny ate a lot of chocolate cake. He was sick.
   Danny _____ sick because he _____ a lot of chocolate cake.

3 Zoe finished her homework. She went out with her friends.
   Zoe _____ her homework when she _____ out with her friends.

4 I read the book in May last year. I saw the film in August last year.
   I _____ the film after I _____ the book.

5 Dad cooked dinner at seven o'clock. Mum got home at eight o'clock.
   By the time Mum _____ home, Dad _____ dinner.

5 Circle the correct words.

1 John **had never tried** / **never tried** Indian food before.

2 I had just got into the bath when the phone **had rung** / **rang**.

3 The cake **had tasted** / **tasted** horrible because Jane had put salt in it instead of sugar!

4 Gran **had put** / **put** the presents under the bed before the children woke up.

5 By the time the police got to the house, the dog **had disappeared** / **disappeared**.

6 **Had you ever seen** / **Did you ever see** a real lion before you went to Africa?

6 Complete the sentences with the past simple or the past perfect simple of the verbs in brackets.

1 By the time the explorer, Jacques-Yves Cousteau, ____died____ (die) in 1997,
   he ____had written____ (write) many books.

2 Norway's Roald Amundsen _____ (already / reach) the South Pole when Englishman
   Captain Scott _____ (arrive) there in 1912.

3 The Vikings _____ (already / discover) North America 500 hundred years before
   Christopher Columbus _____ (sail) there in 1492.

4 Amelia Earhart _____ (break) many world records
   before she _____ (disappear) in 1937.

5 No human being _____ (walk) on the Moon
   before Neil Armstrong _____ (step) out
   of Apollo 11 in 1969.

Lesson 3

1 Circle the correct words.

1 He **fell** / **hid** in the forest because he was scared.

2 Anansi carried a **basket** / **food** around the village.

3 He asked everyone to give him a bit of their **bag** / **wisdom**.

4 Anansi was worried that people might be **jealous** / **angry** of him.

5 Anansi tried to be wise, but without **success** / **ideas**.

2 Rewrite the sentences with the words given in brackets and any other words which are necessary.

SAY IT LIKE THIS!

1 Gary, you forgot to take the rubbish out! (supposed)
Gary ___was supposed to take___ the rubbish out.

2 Sarah wanted to read the legend, but she couldn't find her book. (going)
Sarah _____ the legend, but she couldn't find her book.

3 Children, I didn't want you to put your mythology books away. (supposed)
The children _____ their mythology books away.

4 We hadn't planned to tell him the legend of the lake, but he found out anyway. (going)
We _____ him the legend of the lake, but he found out anyway.

5 Jack's mother told him to brush his teeth, but he forgot. (supposed)
Jack _____ his teeth, but he forgot.

3 Complete the table about yourself. Use a tick (✓) or a cross (✗).

	Supposed to	Going to
go to the park		
clean your teeth		
take dog for a walk		
climb the tree		
wash the dishes		
make lunch		
do homework		
sail a boat		

4 Tell your partner about the things you are and aren't supposed to do and the things you are or aren't going to do.

> I'm going to go to the park.

> I'm not supposed to sleep in class.

30 UNIT 4

5 Read the traditional story from Britain and circle the correct words.

> **Remember!**
>
> We can use these words and phrases to tell a story.
> Once upon a time, At the beginning
> One day / morning / night
> In the end, Finally
> After a while, Suddenly, About an hour later,
> Then, After that, The next thing I knew, Soon

(1) **One day / (Once upon)** a time, there was a poor boy called Dick Whittington. He decided to travel to London where, people said, the streets were made of gold.

(2) **Soon / As soon as** Dick reached London, but he found that the streets were not made of gold. Cold and hungry, he fell asleep on the steps of a big house. It belonged to a rich man called Mr Fitzwarren who gave Dick a job in the kitchen. Dick's room in the house was full of rats so he bought a cat to catch them.

(3) **One day / At first**, Mr Fitzwarren told Dick that one of his ships was sailing to a far-away land. 'Send something of your own on the ship,' he told Dick, 'and I will sell it for some gold.' Dick had nothing else, so he sent his cat.

In the kitchen, the cook was horrible to Dick and he ran away. He had reached the edge of the city when (4) **after that / suddenly** the city bells rang. Dick thought that he heard the words 'Turn back Whittington, Lord Mayor of London!' Dick was amazed and returned. There he found that Mr Fitzwarren's ship had returned. His cat had been sold to a king whose palace was full of mice! The king was very pleased with the cat. Dick had become a rich man, and (5) **in the end / at the beginning** he became Lord Mayor of London!

London

6 Write a traditional story from your country. Use the questions in the plan to help you and don't forget to include words from the Remember! box.

Paragraph 1
Who is the main character?
Where did he / she live?
When did the story happen?

Paragraphs 2 and 3
What happened first?
What happened after that?

Paragraph 4
How did the story end?

Review 2 — Units 3–4

1 Read the text about the Northern Lights.

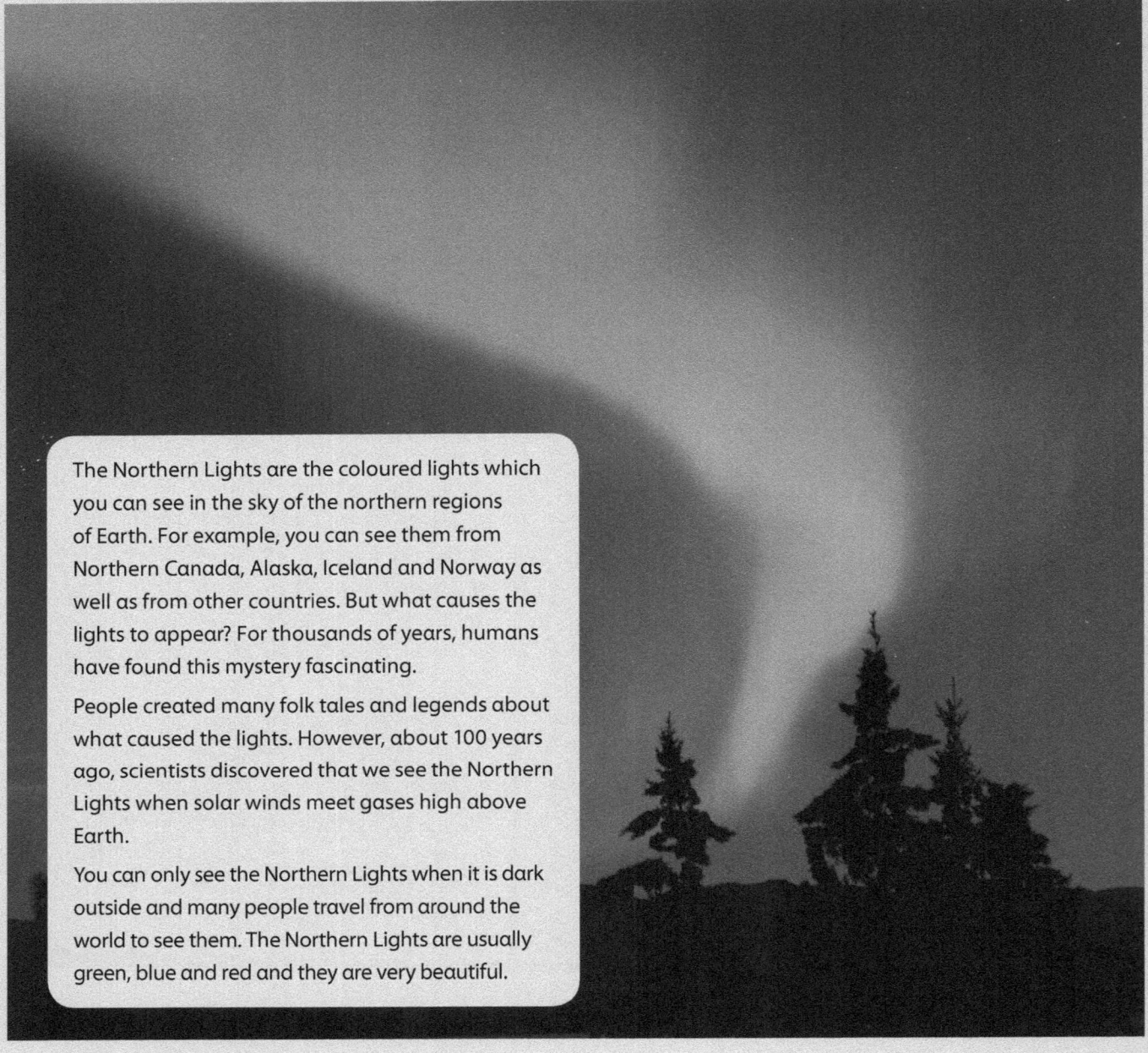

The Northern Lights are the coloured lights which you can see in the sky of the northern regions of Earth. For example, you can see them from Northern Canada, Alaska, Iceland and Norway as well as from other countries. But what causes the lights to appear? For thousands of years, humans have found this mystery fascinating.

People created many folk tales and legends about what caused the lights. However, about 100 years ago, scientists discovered that we see the Northern Lights when solar winds meet gases high above Earth.

You can only see the Northern Lights when it is dark outside and many people travel from around the world to see them. The Northern Lights are usually green, blue and red and they are very beautiful.

2 Answer the questions.

1. Where can you see the Northern Lights? _near the northern regions of Earth_
2. What have people found fascinating for thousands of years? _____
3. How did people explain the Northern Lights in the past? _____
4. What did scientists discover about 100 years ago? _____
5. When can we see the Northern Lights? _____

3 Choose the correct answers.

1. When volcanoes erupt they can cause a lot of _____ .
   a floods
   b pollution
   c droughts

2. It was very _____ to light a fire in the woods!
   a brave
   b foolish
   c honest

3. He had an interview but he didn't get _____ .
   a the job
   b the basket
   c the surprise

4. My brother is interested _____ legends.
   a in
   b for
   c of

5. Ow! Your cat has got very sharp _____ !
   a fur
   b claws
   c paws

6. I got the _____ that the archaeologist was happy about something.
   a impression
   b chance
   c reply

7. There's no _____ that more planes crash in the Bermuda Triangle.
   a emergency
   b damage
   c evidence

8. The rivers are all dry because of the _____ .
   a storm
   b drought
   c flood

9. I believe that Amelia Earhart's plane never _____ on the island.
   a landed
   b got home
   c ran out

10. We are _____ for all the animals on this farm.
    a answer
    b suitable
    c responsible

11. The platypus is an unusual _____ .
    a bill
    b mammal
    c reptile

12. Our plane _____ off at exactly eleven o'clock.
    a went
    b took
    c left

4 Choose the correct answers.

1. _____ has it been raining?
   a For very long
   b When
   c How long

2. She hasn't been feeling very well _____ .
   a recently
   b a long time
   c by then

3. He _____ tropical fish since 2007.
   a studies
   b is studying
   c has been studying

4. How long _____ English?
   a have you been learning
   b did you learn
   c do you learn

5. Maths is _____ lesson at school.
   a interesting than
   b the most interesting
   c most interesting

6. I can understand my biology lessons _____ than my history lessons.
   a easiest
   b more easily
   c too easy

7. This is _____ wildfire in 20 years.
   a the worst
   b worst
   c worse

8. _____ the book before you saw the film?
   a Had you read
   b Have you read
   c Have you been reading

9. They had borrowed the book _____ the library.
   a in
   b from
   c by

10. She _____ the bottles to the recycling centre.
    a has already taken
    b has already been taking
    c already takes

11. I _____ to Peru before last year.
    a have never been
    b had never been
    c never went

12. Our teacher was pleased because we _____ ten trees.
    a plant
    b had planted
    c have planted

5 Ambitions

Lesson 1

1 Complete the dialogue with these words.

~~advert~~   application   experienced   creative   career   diploma

Andrew: Good morning. I saw your (1) _____advert_____ in the newspaper for the gardener's job.
Mrs Hill: Oh yes, hello. Are you (2) _____ in this kind of work?
Andrew: No, not really. I do have a (3) _____ .
Mrs Hill: Can you be (4) _____ with plants and flowers?
Andrew: Yes, I designed my mum's garden and I really want a (5) _____ in garden design.
Mrs Hill: That's good. Well, we'd like to meet you, so can you come for an interview next Monday?
Andrew: Yes, I can.
Mrs Hill: I'm going to send you a(n) (6) _____ . Please fill it in and bring it with you on Monday.
Andrew: All right, thank you very much.

2 Write the missing letters.

1 You study here after you finish school.   u <u>n i v e r s i t y</u>
2 You get this when you finish university.   d _ _ _ _ _ _
3 This is another word for career.   o _ _ _ _ _ _ _ _ _
4 You work for this person.   b _ _ _
5 You need these to get a good job.   q _ _ _ _ _ _ _ _ _ _ _ _ _
6 This is the money you earn when you work.   s _ _ _ _ _

3 Match.

1 He did a course at university.
2 She is a leader in art and design.
3 She works nine hours a day, six days a week.
4 She earns lots of money.
5 He's always on TV and in the newspapers.
6 He has lots of career goals.

a She has a good salary.
b He's famous.
c She's creative.
d He's ambitious.
e She's hard-working.
f He's got a degree.

34 UNIT 5

4 Choose the correct answers.

1. I think I'll get the job.
   - (a) It's my opinion that I'll get the job.
   - b It's certain I'll get the job.

2. I'll phone my boss.
   - a I've just decided to phone her.
   - b I've been planning to phone her all day.

3. Watch out! You're going to crash!
   - a An accident is taking place now.
   - b An accident is going to take place in a few moments.

4. Don't worry! We'll drive you home.
   - a We are offering to drive you home.
   - b We predict that we'll drive you home.

5. My sister is going to study journalism at university.
   - a She is planning to study journalism at university.
   - b She is studying journalism at university now.

5 Circle the correct words.

1. Adrian booked his tickets to South America. He **is going to** / **will** fly to Buenos Aires on May 1st.
2. You don't have the right qualifications – I'm sure you **aren't going to** / **won't** get the job.
3. Gary's journey is very dangerous. I hope he **is going to** / **will** be all right.
4. The exams **are going to** / **will** start next month so I have enough time to study before then.
5. She **is going to** / **will** have a well-paid job by the time she's 30.
6. Look at Jim. He **will** / **is going to** drop those books.

6 Complete the email with the correct form of the future simple or *be going to* and the verbs in brackets.

Dear Helen,
You (1) _won't believe_ (not believe) my news – I (2) _____ (travel) to the rainforest in Brazil on June 22nd! I applied to join an Earthwatch teen team and I was accepted!

This year, the team (3) _____ (help) the project leaders to measure trees, count frogs and lizards and study plants. In our free time, we (4) _____ (go) hiking in the mountains or swimming in nearby rivers. For the whole trip, we (5) _____ (sleep) in tents and there is also an area where we can use the showers and toilets.

I hope the food (6) _____ (be) nice!

Tomorrow, Mum (7) _____ (take) me into town to buy my equipment. I'm so excited!

I'm sure it (8) _____ (be) the most amazing experience!
Bye for now!
Leo

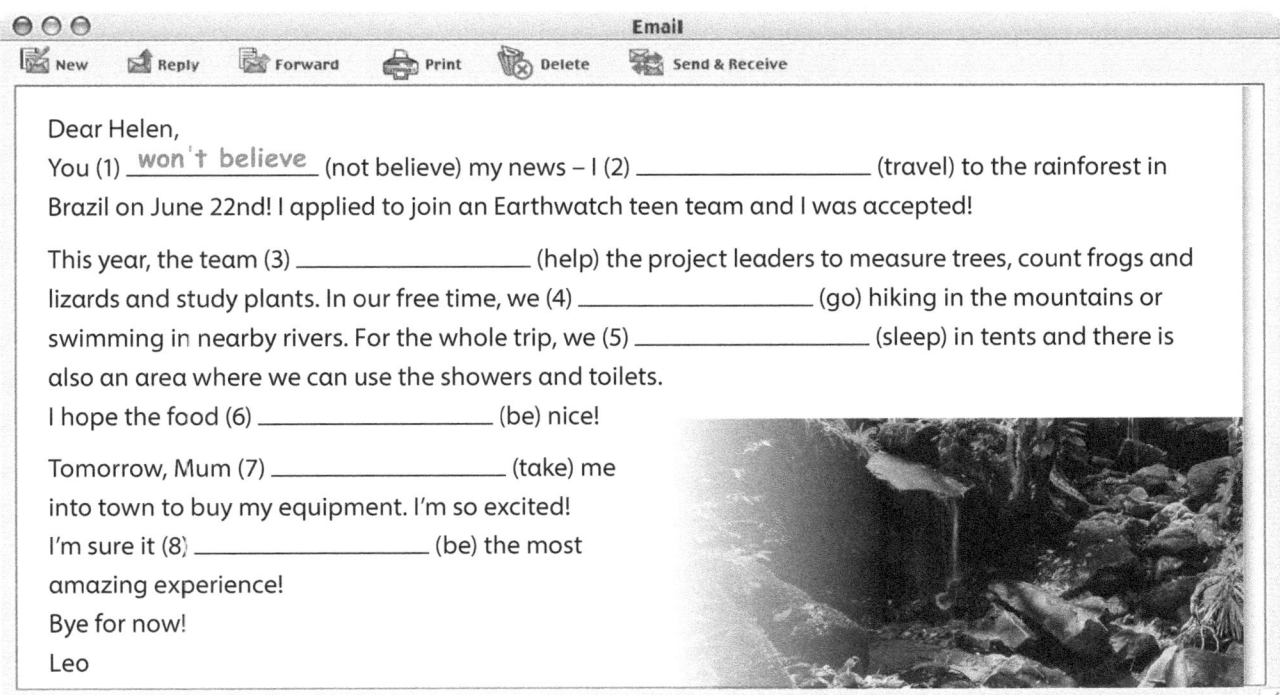

Lesson 2

1 Choose the correct answers.

1 'What is the _____ of talking to a careers officer?'
   'She'll help you decide what you think your perfect job will be.'
   a skill   b contact   (c) purpose

2 Glue is a _____ that sticks things together.
   a substance   b food   c powder

3 Beth is very ambitious. She's _____ to become a famous musician.
   a affected   b determined   c sure

4 This medicine is very _____ for sick dogs.
   a tough   b effective   c disease

5 My daughter is very _____. She never drives dangerously.
   a nice   b bad   c sensible

6 That exam was really _____. Do you think you passed?
   a ambitious   b tough   c delicious

2 The words in bold are in the wrong sentences. Put them in the correct place.

1 The weather might **project** our picnic today.   _affect_

2 University courses **knowledge** you for your career.   _____

3 We want to **inspire** our theory about solar power.   _____

4 My daughter has a very good **prove** of Greek history. _____

5 Famous scientists **affect** children to become scientists, too. _____

6 I want to finish my geography **prepare** this weekend. _____

3 Complete the sentences with these words.

| down   off   ~~over~~   to   up (x2)   with (x2) |

1 Steve caught malaria while he was in South Africa, but he's getting _over_ it now.

2 How do you put up _____ the insects biting you at night?

3 I wanted to go to the nature reserve, but the idea of so many big snakes put me _____!

4 We're nearly at the top of the mountain. We can't give _____ now!

5 I applied for a place on the expedition, but they turned me _____.

6 Slow down! I can't keep _____ with you!

7 We're really looking forward _____ our journey to South Africa.

8 What's the best way to deal _____ insect bites?

36 UNIT 5

4 Complete the sentences with the future continuous of these verbs.

> cycle   do   land   ~~make~~   sail   write

1 The explorers __will be making__ a long journey across the desert.
2 By this time next week, Debbie _____ across the Pacific Ocean.
3 He _____ articles for the newspaper as he travels around South America.
4 This is your pilot speaking. We _____ at Gatwick Airport in six minutes.
5 Dad _____ to his meeting because it's too far to walk.
6 Next week the children _____ a project about the rainforest.

5 Circle the correct words.

1 **(Will we be having)** / **We will be having** roast chicken for lunch on Sunday?
2 **In** / **For** a few years, you will become famous!
3 This time **yesterday** / **tomorrow**, I'll be interviewing Jim Jones, the famous actor. Wish me luck!
4 **During** / **In** the day, Sue works as a waitress.
5 She **stays** / **will be staying** in a five star hotel next week.
6 I'll be studying **yesterday** / **tomorrow** so I can't come on the trip.

6 Look at the diary and complete the sentences with the future continuous.

Monday	fly to San Juan, Puerto Rico
Tuesday	take bus to Guanica
Wednesday	buy food and equipment for the expedition
Thursday	hike to campsite in rainforest
Friday	put up tents – me, set up GPS unit – Larry
Saturday	have a rest

1 On Monday, we __will be flying__ to San Juan in Puerto Rico.
2 On Tuesday, we _____ the bus to Guanica.
3 At this time on Wednesday, we _____ food and equipment for the expedition.
4 On Thursday, we _____ to our campsite in the rainforest.
5 At this time on Friday, I _____ our tents and Larry _____ the GPS unit.
6 On Saturday, we _____ a rest!

Lesson 3

1 Choose the correct answers.

1 wealthy
   - (a) rich
   - b lucky

2 foreign country
   - a your own country
   - b a country which is different from yours

3 original
   - a interesting
   - b new

4 hero
   - a somebody you hate
   - b somebody you admire

5 normal
   - a usual
   - b strange

6 talent
   - a special ability
   - b a waste of time

2 Rewrite the sentences. Use the future perfect.

1 Jenny is finishing her report on students' ambitions. She must give it to her boss on Monday morning.
   By Monday morning, Jenny _will have finished her report on students' ambitions_.

2 There are five books in the series and I have read four of them. Mum is going to buy me the last book for my birthday.
   Soon I _____ all the books in the series.

3 It's the beginning of June. I'm going to graduate from university by this time next year!
   By this time next year, I _____!

4 On August 5th, he will start working for the new company.
   By August 6th, he _____.

5 Dad has just cut the grass, but it grows very fast and will soon be long again.
   In one week, the grass _____ again.

6 Our shop is closing in one hour. We won't sell all these shirts before we close.
   We _____ before we close the shop.

3 Look at the pictures and complete the sentences with *be about to* and these verbs.

SAY IT LIKE THIS!

> interview   leave   listen   play   say   wash

1 Mr Hill _is about to interview_ the student.

2 Jimmy _____ his guitar.

3 The boys _____ the car.

4 He _____ the winner's name.

5 They _____ the house.

6 She _____ to her MP3 player.

38 UNIT 5

4 Read the article and choose the best topic sentence for each paragraph. Be careful – there is one sentence you don't need.

Remember!

Each paragraph of your writing should begin with a topic sentence which tells us what the paragraph is about. The rest of the paragraph must follow logically from the topic sentence.

A   Harry practises his basketball skills every day.
B   I'm sure that Harry will succeed in getting into one of the big teams.
C   Harry, who is my best friend, is the most energetic person I know.
D   Harry is very good at sports and his dream has always been to become a footballer.

(1) __C__ He plays basketball, football and tennis. He rides twenty kilometres on his bike every weekend and still has time to do his homework and play with his friends!

(2) _____ Football is his favourite sport. He's the best player in the area and last year he was made captain of the school team. Although he is great fun to be with and we always laugh and joke around, he is very serious about his ambitions. He belongs to the local team and he practises for three hours every Saturday and Sunday.

(3) _____ He is going to start training with Manchester United Academy next September and I believe that he will soon amaze the coach with his skills. I think that he will soon be playing for the team and maybe even scoring goals for England!

5 Write an article about your best friend's ambitions and dreams.

Paragraph 1
Describe your best friend and his / her abilities.

Paragraph 2
Say what his / her goal is and say how he / she is trying to achieve that goal.

Paragraph 3
Make a prediction about whether your friend will succeed.

6 Remarkable People

Lesson 1

1 Complete the sentences with these words.

> adapt   biology   expedition   ~~objected~~   observed   religions   voyages

1 Sam's family __objected__ to him studying art. They wanted him to study science.
2 I want to study _____ at university, because I am interested in living things.
3 People follow many different _____ around the world.
4 Charles Darwin _____ nature all his life.
5 Next year, I'm going on an exciting _____ to some mountains in China.
6 Darwin's theory was that animals _____ over time.
7 How many _____ to South Africa have you been on?

2 Write the missing letters.

1 This person wants to work in the government and manage the country.   p o l i t i c i a n
2 This person is interested in living things.   b _ _ _ _ _ _ _
3 This person writes articles or stories for their job.   w _ _ _ _ _
4 This is a person who can sing or play an instrument.   m _ _ _ _ _ _
5 This person works with people who need help with the law.   l _ _ _ _ _
6 This is a person who does a lot of sport.   a _ _ _ _ _ _ _

3 Choose the correct answers.

1 Only two ____ were chosen to do the research.
   a scientists
   b sciences
2 Andy, who studied ____, works for a big company.
   a biologist
   b biology
3 Who is your favourite ____ ?
   a writing
   b writer
4 He decided to study music instead of ____ .
   a religion
   b research
5 The ____ won his case in court.
   a law
   b lawyer
6 Kerry is a talented ____ ; she plays the piano and the violin really well.
   a musician
   b music

40 UNIT 6

4 Circle the correct words.

1 Kate is really interested in **observing** / **to observe** wildlife.
2 He used to **spend** / **spending** all his free time exploring nature.
3 **To study** / **Studying** plant specimens is his favourite pastime.
4 Do you enjoy **to watch** / **watching** documentaries?
5 I promise **bringing** / **to bring** back your book about fossils tomorrow.
6 Did you manage **to complete** / **completing** your chemistry homework in time?

5 Look at the pictures and complete the sentences with the gerund or infinitive form of these verbs.

> buy   draw   ~~listen~~   paint   wake up   windsurf

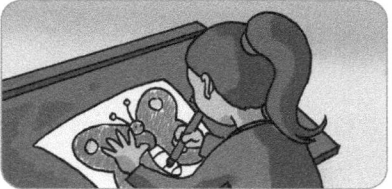

1 Mary has just started ___listening___ to her favourite song.
3 James learnt _____ at the age of seven.
5 Alice is really good at _____ insects.

2 Jack always goes _____ in the summer.
4 I can't afford _____ that dress.
6 My dad is a postman so he's used to _____ early in the morning.

6 Complete the article with the gerund or infinitive form of the verbs in brackets.

Dian Fossey was an American zoologist* who was famous for (1) ___living___ (live) with gorillas in the jungles of Africa. (2) _____ (Become) a zoologist was not always what she had planned to do, though. Before (3) _____ (travel) to Africa she used (4) _____ (work) at a children's hospital in Kentucky.

She first became interested in (5) _____ (go) to Africa when her friend showed her some photos from the area. Another scientist, Dr Louis Leakey, asked her (6) _____ (do) some research on the mountain gorillas of Rwanda. With his help she managed (7) _____ (raise) enough money to begin her research.

In 1967, she set up camp in the rain forest of Rwanda where she spent 18 years trying (8) _____ (save) mountain gorillas from extinction. Today, The Gorilla Organisation continues to protect gorillas in their natural habitat.

*someone who studies animals

Lesson 2

1 Complete the sentences with the correct form of *give* or *take*.

1 My teacher ____*gave*____ me some great advice about what course to study.
2 I saw a photo which _____ me a great idea for a story.
3 I can't come out tonight because I've got to _____ care of my little sister.
4 It _____ a long time to invent the gadget.
5 Can you _____ me a lift home, please?
6 Why don't you _____ me a ring later?
7 You should _____ your mother's advice and study harder.
8 Amy wants to _____ part in an expedition to Brazil.

2 Complete the sentences with these words.

| achievement | ~~admire~~ | adopted | appear | extraordinary | medals |

1 I really ____*admire*____ my sister, because she follows her dreams.
2 Athletes want to win gold _____ in competitions.
3 My greatest _____ is getting into university.
4 Our dad is an _____ musician. He has played with famous pop stars.
5 My uncle and aunt have _____ two children.
6 Sam's dream is to _____ on television one day.

3 Circle the correct words.

1 It was **for** / **(by)** chance that I found tickets – they were very hard to find!
2 I'm sorry I forgot to get you an autograph – I didn't do it **on** / **with** purpose, you know.
3 I left school **at** / **on** the age of 16 and I started work in a supermarket.
4 Bob lost his job last May and has been **out** / **away** of work ever since.
5 Tim was **on** / **in** his twenties when he first took part in the Olympic Games.
6 I've wanted to see a Shakespeare play **in** / **for** ages! Thanks for the tickets!

4 Write *S* if the sentences have the same meaning and *D* if they are different.

1. ☐ S
   I started to go to the library.
   I started going to the library.

2. ☐
   He stopped to sign my book.
   He stopped signing my book.

3. ☐
   They remembered leaving home at six o'clock.
   They remembered to leave home at six o'clock.

4. ☐
   She continued to read the book.
   She continued reading the book.

5. ☐
   I like to see documentaries about remarkable people.
   I like seeing documentaries about remarkable people.

6. ☐
   They went on to invent special gadgets in the 1990s.
   They went on inventing special gadgets in the 1990s.

5 Choose the correct answers.

1. Try adding some salt to the soup.
   a) Why don't you add some salt to the soup?
   b) It's difficult to add salt to the soup.

2. Have you forgotten coming to my house before?
   a) Can't you remember that you were at my house before?
   b) Did you forget to come to my house before?

3. We need to stop to buy some water.
   a) We mustn't buy any more water.
   b) Let's buy some water.

4. She remembered to meet her aunt at the train station.
   a) She remembered the time she met her aunt at the train station.
   b) She didn't forget to go and meet her aunt at the train station.

5. They started singing the song and everyone clapped.
   a) They began to sing the song and the other people clapped.
   b) The other people clapped after they sang the song.

6. She stopped crying and started to run to school.
   a) She didn't cry any more and began to run to school.
   b) She stopped and cried and didn't run to school.

6 Circle the correct words.

1. She never stopped **practising** / **to practise** the violin. She really loved it.
2. The actor has gone on **becoming** / **to become** famous worldwide.
3. He remembered **taking** / **to take** part in the Marathon many years ago.
4. You forgot **to wake** / **waking** me up this morning. I was late for work!
5. Why don't you try **to listen** / **listening** to the radio?

Lesson 3

1 Complete the crossword puzzle.

Down

1. You feel like this when you feel very happy because of something you have done.
2. This is a situation in which people try to win.
3. This means to finish something.
4. You win this. It could be money, a cup or something else.

Across

3. This tells you how to cook things.
6. You are very good at something when you are this.

2 Put the words in the correct order to make sentences.

SAY IT LIKE THIS!

1. competition / too / is / it / see / late / to / the
   It is too late to see the competition.

2. it / today / warm / swim / enough / isn't / to / outside

3. excited / are / too / down / they / sit / to

4. too / he / watch / tired / to / TV / is

5. the / is / fly / strong / the / kite / enough / to / wind

6. isn't / the / film / old / to / she / enough / see

3 Read the comments and talk to your partner about the party. Use *too* and *enough*.

Mary's party was terrible! Her living room was crowded with people and it was really noisy.

There was pizza to eat, but it was cold.

There was ice cream for dessert, but it was warm!

The games were really silly so we didn't play – they were for babies!

Tim brought a film for us to watch. It was supposed to be a comedy, but it wasn't funny so we didn't watch it.

4 Complete the email with these words and phrases.

~~although~~   apart from   but   however

Remember!

We can use these linking words to add information.
both ... and, as well as ..., apart from ..., in addition ...
We can use these linking words to contrast two different ideas.
... but ..., although ..., ... whereas ..., however, ...

Dear *Brave Kids*,

I'm writing to tell you about my friend Philip. He's the bravest boy I know and I think he should win the *Bravest Child of the Month* prize. His friends and family are all very proud of him.

Ten-year-old Philip was born with a disease which means that he is always breaking his bones. (1) **Although** he has a serious illness, Philip loves playing sports and in January last year he started wheelchair racing. (2) _____ his first race, in which he came second, Philip has won every other race since then! Looking for a new challenge, Philip decided to take part in the London Wheelchair Marathon. (3) _____, five days before the race Philip got sick. Determined to take part, Philip was given medicine by his doctor and guess what? He not only completed the marathon, (4) _____ he also finished in first place!

Philip is both determined and brave and that's why I hope you will choose him to be the *Bravest Child of the Month*.

Best wishes,

Joe

5 Write an email to *Brave Kids* about a child you know who is very brave and who you think should win the *Bravest Child of the Month* prize.

Begin like this:
Dear *Brave Kids*,

Paragraph 1
Introduce the person you are going to describe.

Paragraph 2
Explain why he / she is brave and describe his / her achievements and how he / she faced his / her problems.

Paragraph 3
Sum up why you think he / she should win the prize for *Bravest Child of the Month*.

Finish like this:
Best wishes,
(your name)

Review 3 — Units 5–6

1 Read the text about rock climbing.

Rock climbing is a popular hobby that many people enjoy doing. (1) __c__ It is fun and it also helps people deal with stress.

(2) _____ They need to be half a size smaller than your usual size. The next thing you need is a harness. (3) _____ It's important to know how to use your equipment. (4) _____ A climber with experience can help you a lot in the beginning.

Rock climbing is very exciting for both adults and kids who like a challenge. Climbers, however, must be careful not to do damage to the environment. Sometimes rock climbers leave rubbish on the mountains where they climb. (5) _____ This will allow future climbers to enjoy a clean, natural environment which has not been destroyed by pollution.

2 Complete the text with these sentences.

a   This allows you to move freely, but will hold you up if you fall.

b   If you are a beginner, it's best to have lessons.

c   You can do it indoors on special walls or outdoors on real mountains.

d   The most important thing to have is good shoes.

e   They should take it with them and throw it away.

3 Choose the correct answers.

1 My boss is very _____. She works hard.
   a ambitious
   b creative
   c nice

2 You need to have excellent _____ to work there.
   a qualifications
   b experiences
   c research

3 Most _____ are looking for hard-working students.
   a workers
   b salaries
   c universities

4 We're only interested in inventors with _____ ideas.
   a extraordinary
   b famous
   c normal

5 The _____ by boat took six weeks.
   a travel
   b voyage
   c ride

6 He was _____ his forties when he met my mother.
   a on
   b in
   c as

7 I applied for the job but they _____ me down.
   a turned
   b put
   c cut

8 Please fill in the _____.
   a qualifications
   b application
   c interview

9 The _____ won the race yesterday.
   a athlete
   b gardener
   c journalist

10 He loved to sing and dance and became a _____.
   a musician
   b biologist
   c writer

11 I'm going to be late. Can you _____ me a lift?
   a take
   b bring
   c give

12 You have to be _____ to survive alone in the rain forest.
   a interested
   b glamorous
   c tough

4 Choose the correct answers.

1 I'm sure you _____ a place at university.
   a are getting
   b are going to get
   c will get

2 My class _____ the Science Museum next weekend.
   a is going to visit
   b had visited
   c will have visited

3 _____ to university next year?
   a You are going
   b Will you be going
   c Do you go

4 _____ buy me a book about volcanoes, please?
   a Will you
   b Are you going to
   c Do you

5 The explorers _____ the North Pole by the end of June.
   a have reached
   b will have reached
   c will reaching

6 This time next week, we _____ the whole rainforest.
   a will have explored
   b will have been exploring
   c have explored

7 Next month, he _____ round Italy.
   a travels
   b will have travelled
   c will be travelling

8 You forgot _____ the car door again. It's still open.
   a locking
   b to lock
   c locked

9 _____ volcanoes is a very dangerous job!
   a Studying
   b To study
   c Study

10 I decided _____ Mike, who is working in Canada.
   a email
   b emailing
   c to email

11 I remember _____ you put the tickets in your bag.
   a to have seen
   b seeing
   c to see

12 He refused _____ his ambition of climbing Mount Everest.
   a to give up
   b giving up
   c give up

7 Body and Mind

Lesson 1

1 Match.

1. taste — d
2. sound
3. sight
4. touch
5. smell

a you use your nose for this
b you use your ears for this
c you use your eyes for this
d you use your mouth for this
e you use your hands for this

2 Circle the correct words.

1. Tennis is a (physical) / muscle activity.
2. I don't feel sensible / energetic if I sleep badly.
3. I was very emotional / tough when my sister left for university.
4. Exams bring lots of time / stress to students.
5. My muscles are often easy / sore after running.
6. Taste is one of the five senses / feelings.

3 Write the missing letters.

1. It's important to eat a healthy d i e t.
2. When you feel happy in a place you feel c _ _ _ _ _ _ _ _ _ _.
3. If you put your m _ _ _ to it, you will succeed.
4. When you break your arm you are in p _ _ _ .
5. Before a test you can feel nervous and t _ _ _ _ _.
6. If you exercise every day you will be healthy and f _ _ .
7. Don't forget to b _ _ _ _ _ _ when you are stressed!

48 UNIT 7

4 Choose the correct answers.

1 He can leave it here …
   a for five minutes. *(circled)*
   b until he came back.

2 She could cook very well …
   a with less practice.
   b when I knew her.

3 He could play sports …
   a by 7 p.m.
   b when he was young.

4 We can finish our project …
   a next week.
   b last week.

5 She can play the piano …
   a when her arm is better.
   b a few years ago.

6 We couldn't find it …
   a until tomorrow.
   b when we looked for it.

5 Complete the sentences with the correct form of *be able to* and the verbs in brackets.

1 I'm sorry but I ___haven't been able to find___ (find) your dog yet.
2 I _____ (unlock) the door. I think this must be the wrong key.
3 Mary _____ (give) Jean any advice because she didn't know what to say.
4 _____ (Jack / leave) the hospital tomorrow afternoon?
5 I _____ (come) to football practice tomorrow because I have a dentist's appointment.
6 She _____ (play) the piano when she was just four years old. She was very good!

6 Look at the pictures and write *T* for (True) and *F* for (False).

1 The girl is able to run faster than the boy. [F]
2 Most people can't eat this. ☐
3 She isn't able to cycle to the gym. ☐
4 This girl is able to ride her bike. ☐
5 He can go to school. ☐
6 She was able to win the race. ☐

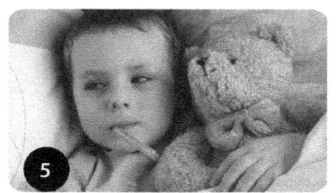

Lesson 2

1 Circle the odd one out.

1 anxious • tense • (satisfied)
2 memory • suffer • pain
3 brain • arm • benefit
4 depressed • happy • negative
5 positive • belong • self-confident

2 Choose the correct answers.

1 'Excuse me. Could I try ___ these football boots, please?'
   'Yes, of course.'
   a in
   (b) on
   c off

2 My favourite film company has just brought ___ a documentary about the brain.
   a out
   b over
   c off

3 You should always put your helmet ___ before you cycle.
   a on
   b off
   c up

4 'This new exercise bike really caught ___ this year.'
   'Yes. I'm going to buy one too.'
   a up
   b on
   c over

5 'Take ___ your coat and hat and put them on that chair.'
   'Can I put my umbrella there too?'
   a on
   b up
   c off

3 Circle the correct words.

1 Studying hard **produces** / **benefits** good exam results.
2 Regular exercise helps you to stay **positive** / **negative**.
3 There are lots of people who **live** / **suffer** from pain in the world.
4 Going hiking improves my **mood** / **brain**.
5 People who are less **active** / **interested** are more likely to feel depressed.
6 If you are **self-confident** / **negative**, you feel good about yourself.
7 Deniz is a great footballer and she **belongs** / **breathes** in our team.
8 Your **memories** / **muscles** are the things you've done that you remember.

50 UNIT 7

4 Complete the sentences with *must* or *can't*.

1 That man is wearing a suit and tie. He ___must___ be the shop manager.

2 This _____ be Mum's tennis racket; you know she hates tennis.

3 That _____ be Carl; he won't be back from Egypt until Friday.

4 Those are really nice trainers. They _____ be very expensive.

5 She _____ know a lot about health; she buys four health magazines every week!

6 Mario _____ be very happy; he looks depressed every day.

5 Circle the correct words.

1 Kelly **must** / (**might**) enjoy playing ice hockey; let's invite her, too.

2 Christine **must** / **may** be very positive; she's always smiling and laughing.

3 This **can't** / **might not** be a hospital; there aren't any doctors here!

4 **May be** / **May** I try on this dress?

5 They **can't** / **may not** have time to visit the museum.

6 Andy **may be** / **maybe** anxious about his exams.

6 Choose the correct answers.

Hala: Mum said that she (1) ____ buy me some new hiking boots at the weekend if she has time to go shopping.

Jade: Oh, that's nice. She (2) ____ be happy with you for some reason.

Hala: Well, yes, she is. She was really pleased with my exam results. She (3) ____ buy me some new trainers, too! It's good to benefit from all that hard work.

Jade: I've seen some fantastic trainers at Sports World. They're silver and pink. I think they were designed by a famous athlete though, so they (4) ____ cost a lot of money.

Hala: But Sports World only sells cheap clothes and shoes. Those trainers you saw (5) ____ be expensive.

Jade: Well, why don't you ask your mum to take you there on Saturday? You never know – you (6) ____ find some other things you like, too.

1 a must   (b) might   c can't
2 a might   b can't   c must
3 a can't   b maybe   c may
4 a must   b can   c might not
5 a may   b can't   c must
6 a might   b must   c can

Lesson 3

1 Complete the sentences with these words.

> exhausted   ~~hurt~~   terrible   upset   go   helpful

1. Bob really __hurt__ my feelings when he said my clothes were ugly.
2. I think Sara is _____ after playing basketball all day.
3. My brother often cleans the house and waters the plants. He's very _____ .
4. I'm _____ because my best friend has moved to Australia.
5. Maria is _____ at art, but she's very good at maths.
6. If you let _____ of your negative thoughts, you will be more self-confident.

2 Rewrite the sentences with the words given in brackets and any other words that are necessary.

1. Doing more exercise is a good idea. (should)
   You __should do__ more exercise.
2. Don't eat so many snacks. (must)
   You _____ so many snacks.
3. It's important that you clean your teeth every morning. (ought)
   You _____ your teeth every morning.
4. It isn't necessary to go to school today. (have)
   We _____ to school today.
5. It isn't necessary for Stella to take the pills. (doesn't)
   Stella _____ the pills if she doesn't want to.
6. You have to eat less food if you want to lose weight. (must)
   You _____ less food if you want to lose weight.

3 Look at the pictures and write the correct sentences.

SAY IT LIKE THIS!

> Do you think I should join?   ~~We'd better not touch them.~~
> What do you think I should wear?   Why don't you cycle to school?

1. We'd better not touch them.
2. _____
3. _____
4. _____

52   UNIT 7

4 Read the letter and answer the questions.

Dear Robyn,
My mother recently had a beautiful baby boy. He's really sweet and never cries or wakes up in the night. The problem is that my mum and dad spend all their time with the baby. Nobody ever has any time for me. When I come home from school my mum is always busy with the baby – even my friends spend all their time with the baby when they come to my house! So now I feel sad instead of happy about my baby brother. What should I do?
Clare, 12

Remember!

We can use these phrases to ask for advice.
What should I do?
Please tell me how I can …

We can use these phrases to give advice.
I suggest that you should …
Why don't you …?

We can use these phrases to end a letter of advice.
I hope you are able to …
I'm sure you will …
Good luck!

1 What is Clare's problem?
   Her mum and dad spend all their time with the baby.

2 What happens when she comes home from school?

3 What do her friends do when they visit her house?

4 What advice could you give her?

5 Write a reply to the letter in Activity 4, giving advice to Clare. Don't forget to use the phrases in the Remember! box for giving advice. Use this plan to help you.

Begin like this:
Dear Clare,

Paragraph 1
Talk about your own experience or a friend's in the same situation.

Paragraph 2
Say what Clare should do – use your ideas from Activity 4.

Paragraph 3
Wish her luck in solving her problem.

End like this:
Good luck,
(your name)

8 The Arts

Lesson 1

1 Match.

1. portrait — e
2. landscape
3. contrast
4. exhibition
5. frame
6. flash

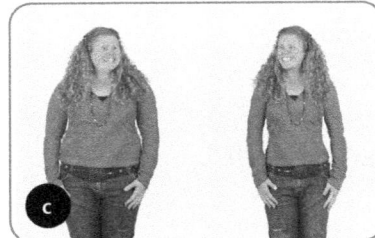

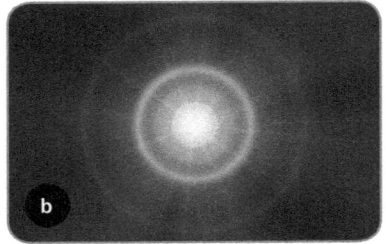

2 Complete the sentences with these words.

abandoned   copy   permission   mural   scenes   community

1. 'Guerilla gardeners' plant flowers or crops in __abandoned__ areas.
2. Did you get _____ before you took that sandwich?
3. There's a beautiful new _____ painted on our school wall.
4. There are lots of people who do yarn-bombing in our _____ .
5. My dad has just bought a _____ of a famous painting.
6. The exhibition showed _____ of life in Athens.

3 Circle the correct words.

1. This sculpture isn't **original** / **new**, it's a copy!
2. The wall was **scary** / **dull** before she painted the mural on it.
3. Is there a **public** / **closed** park in your town where we can plant a sunflower?
4. I have a friend who does **graffiti** / **permission** on street signs at night.
5. Our town is not very **sophisticated** / **abandoned**, but it does have one good art gallery.
6. Is this an original **landscape** / **portrait** of your mother?

54 UNIT 8

4 Complete the museum leaflet with the present simple passive of the verbs in brackets.

Museum of Modern Art

Welcome to the Museum of Modern Art. Please take some time to read this leaflet before you begin your tour.

- Visitors (1) __are reminded__ (remind) to leave their bags and coats at the information desk.
- Taking photos (2) _____ (not allow).
- The paintings (3) _____ (place) in order according to when they were painted.
- All the rubbish at The Museum of Modern Art (4) _____ (recycle) and no energy (5) _____ (waste).
- Many members of the community (6) _____ (involve) in working as volunteers at the museum. Ask at the ticket office for details.

Enjoy your visit!

5 Rewrite the sentences with the words given in brackets and any other words that are necessary.

1 Vincent van Gogh painted 'Sunflowers'. (by)
 'Sunflowers' __was painted by__ Vincent van Gogh.

2 They didn't tell us that the art gallery was closed. (were)
 We _____ that the art gallery was closed.

3 A farmer found an ancient sculpture on his land. (by)
 An ancient sculpture _____ a farmer on his land.

4 Unfortunately, the judges didn't choose my entry. (was)
 Unfortunately, my entry _____ the judges.

5 The fire damaged two paintings at the museum. (were)
 Two paintings _____ by fire at the museum.

6 Choose the correct answers.

1 This photo was ____ when we were on holiday in North Wales.
 a take
 (b) taken
 c took

2 We ____ invited to stay here by my aunt.
 a were
 b was
 c is

3 It ____ built 200 years ago!
 a weren't
 b wasn't
 c isn't

4 We were taught how to paint landscapes ____ our teacher.
 a of
 b when
 c by

5 I ____ expected to audition for the play next week.
 a is
 b are
 c am

6 Were the best pop songs ____ by The Beatles?
 a sing
 b sung
 c sang

Lesson 2

1 Complete the crossword puzzle.

Down

1. Rubbish was the neighbourhood's only r_esource_ to make instruments.
2. My parents are p_____ of my qualifications.
3. I want to d_____ a musical instrument to my school.
4. How can we m_____ Azra to exercise more?

Across

5. I've got the o_____ to study in London next year.
6. Samantha is a new r_____ of this town.

2 Circle the correct answers.

1. Listening to music has an amazing effect **on** / **in** the baby.
2. We're trying to come **out** / **up** with a name for our new band.
3. Adrian is an expert **with** / **on** classical music.
4. Do you think we can change the students' attitude **to** / **for** exams?
5. I like Taylor Swift, but I'm not a lover **of** / **to** pop music.
6. There's no need **of** / **for** more light. It's very bright.
7. We've run out **to** / **of** sugar, so I can't make the cake.

3 Write I (Musical Instruments), P (Performers) or S (Song-related words).

1. sing — S
2. violin
3. singer
4. orchestra
5. tune
6. saxophone
7. compose
8. piano player
9. cello
10. musician
11. guitar
12. dancer

56 UNIT 8

4 Choose the correct answers.

1 Songs _____ for the new album.
   a were being produced (circled)
   b were producing

2 The new piano _____ tomorrow morning.
   a hasn't been delivered
   b won't be delivered

3 Have the prizes already been _____ out?
   a give
   b given

4 Tickets for the concert _____ at the information centre.
   a can be bought
   b you can buy

5 The winners of the talent contest _____ a place at music college.
   a will be offered
   b will they offer

6 Classical music _____ by the orchestra now.
   a wasn't being played
   b is being played

5 Write sentences with the correct form of the passive voice.

1 her new album / record / at the moment
   Her new album is being recorded at the moment.

2 ? / the book / make / into a film
   _____

3 live music / play / at the party / next week
   _____

4 all musical instruments / must / return / to Mrs Hill
   _____

5 the room / paint / at eight o'clock / yesterday
   _____

6 the winner / not choose / yet
   _____

6 Complete the web page with the correct form of the verbs in brackets in the passive voice.

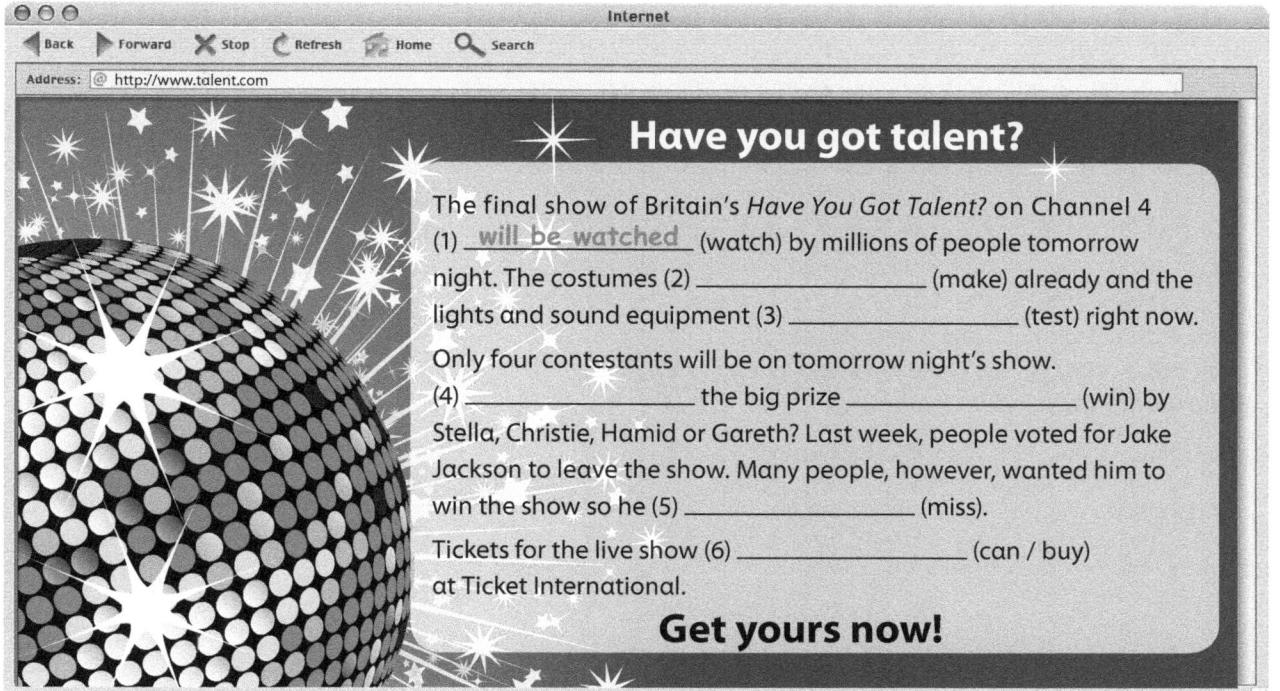

Have you got talent?

The final show of Britain's *Have You Got Talent?* on Channel 4 (1) _will be watched_ (watch) by millions of people tomorrow night. The costumes (2) _____ (make) already and the lights and sound equipment (3) _____ (test) right now.
Only four contestants will be on tomorrow night's show. (4) _____ the big prize _____ (win) by Stella, Christie, Hamid or Gareth? Last week, people voted for Jake Jackson to leave the show. Many people, however, wanted him to win the show so he (5) _____ (miss).
Tickets for the live show (6) _____ (can / buy) at Ticket International.

Get yours now!

Lesson 3

1 Circle the correct words.

1 The actors were wearing fascinating **costumes** / designs in the play.
2 Peter must be good at **sewing** / **working**. He makes all his own clothes.
3 Every **audition** / **detail** is important when you are designing historical costumes.
4 We have a lot of people on our design **team** / **career**.
5 What **pieces** / **materials** did you use for that dress?
6 It's important to **plan** / **see** a new costume carefully.

2 Look at the pictures and write questions.

SAY IT LIKE THIS!

1 ? / what / the opera / like
What was the opera like?

2 ? / what / it like / to be / 80

3 ? / what / you / think of / the London Eye

4 ? / what / you / think of / the play

5 ? / what / your sandwich / like

3 Work with a partner. Take it in turns to tell each other what things have or haven't been done before the exhibition opening.

door / fix
floors / clean
flowers / buy
food / put on table
paintings / put up
windows / wash

58 UNIT 8

4 Look at the two paragraph plans for a review. Which one is better?

A ☐

Paragraph 1 – name of show, name of writer, names of all the actors and singers

Paragraph 2 – detailed descriptions of each scene in the show

Paragraph 3 – reasons why you didn't enjoy the show

Paragraph 4 – description of the setting and costumes

Remember !

Before you begin writing you should:
- decide how many paragraphs you are going to write
- make notes on what you are going to include in each paragraph

B

Paragraph 1 – name of show, when you saw it, name of theatre

Paragraph 2 – general information about the show

Paragraph 3 – focus on one or two things about the show (the acting / the music / the costumes / other)

Paragraph 4 – recommendation

5 Read the review and put the paragraphs in the correct order. Then decide which of the two paragraph plans the writer has used.

☐ 4

I recommend Princess Wishes to anyone who wants a fantastic night out for all the family. Children and adults will love it and at the end of the evening you won't want to go home!

My family and I went to see Disney on Ice: Princess Wishes two weeks ago at the Grand Arena. It was a brilliant experience!

The best thing about the show was the dancing. The performers were skating so quickly that they seemed to be flying! Wearing their classic Disney costumes, they all looked amazing! I especially enjoyed Jasmine's part of the show which was set in a beautiful palace.

Disney on Ice makes the famous Disney characters look alive in a show where all the performers are ice skaters! In Princess Wishes each part of the performance is based on one of Disney's famous princesses – Ariel, Elsa, Anna, Mulan, Belle, Snow White and Sleeping Beauty. This amazing show is a combination of ice dancing, music and magic!

6 Write a review of a play or musical which you have seen. Before you begin your writing make a plan with notes for each paragraph. Refer to the correct plan in Activity 4.

Review 4 — Units 7–8

1 Read the text about a museum.

The Milwaukee Museum of Modern Art is more than just a building – it is a work of art! A new part of the museum, created by Santiago Calatrava, was completed in 2001. It is called the Quadracci Pavilion and it was considered so great that Time Magazine named it 'Best Design of 2001'. This is because it is not only beautiful, but useful as well.

In the Quadracci Pavilion, there are two enormous 'wings' which open and close twice a day. It takes 3.5 minutes for them to open or close. When the 'wings' are open, they are as wide as the wings of a large aeroplane – a little more than 66 metres long. This new part of the museum includes a theatre, a café, a shop, plus a huge space for exhibitions and much more.

The museum is situated in the city on the edge of Lake Michigan in the USA. It has become a landmark and symbol of the city of Milwaukee. Both locals and visitors love it.

2 Write *T* (True) or *F* (False).

1. Santiago Calatrava was born in 2001. — F
2. The 'wings' are as wide as those of a small aeroplane. ☐
3. There are 66 Quadracci Pavilions. ☐
4. There is a café and a shop in the new part of the museum. ☐
5. The museum is in the city of Milwaukee. ☐

3 Choose the correct answers.

1 Regular exercise keeps _____ strong.
   a brains
   b pain
   c muscles

2 Sue's idea for a school health club has really _____ on!
   a caught
   b run
   c taken

3 We saw some beautiful paintings at the _____ .
   a performance
   b interview
   c exhibition

4 I'm more _____ after my good exam results.
   a self-confident
   b negative
   c tense

5 Remember to _____ when you are stressed or upset.
   a motivate
   b breathe
   c perform

6 I plan to donate this money to the local _____ .
   a mural
   b landscapes
   c community

7 Tom stepped on my toe and now it's really _____ .
   a stressed
   b sore
   c calm

8 Dan was _____ when he heard the news.
   a emotional
   b exhausted
   c abandoned

9 Are you a _____ of this building?
   a resident
   b violin
   c benefit

10 This room is nice and _____ .
   a anxious
   b comfortable
   c depressed

11 He has really changed his attitude _____ life!
   a at
   b to
   c on

12 Channel 9 is _____ out a new sitcom next month.
   a catching
   b taking
   c bringing

4 Choose the correct answers.

1 _____ to get tickets for the art exhibition?
   a Can you
   b Could you
   c Were you able

2 Stella _____ eat her lunch because she felt ill.
   a isn't able to
   b can't
   c wasn't able to

3 Loud music _____ be played after eleven o'clock.
   a could
   b mustn't
   c must

4 I like all the dresses in the shop, but I think I _____ try on this blue one.
   a might
   b can't
   c was able to

5 Those _____ be my glasses – mine are purple.
   a can't
   b mustn't
   c might not

6 She _____ love reading. She has so many books!
   a can
   b might
   c must

7 We _____ go out – we can stay in and watch a DVD.
   a couldn't
   b mustn't
   c don't have to

8 You _____ look both ways before you cross the street.
   a ought
   b should
   c shouldn't

9 The huge statue _____ by an American artist.
   a was created
   b created
   c create

10 A wonderful exhibition _____ at this time of year.
   a have always put on
   b they always put on
   c is always put on

11 Who was this photo taken _____ ?
   a in
   b by
   c at

12 The music _____ by a famous orchestra.
   a is being played
   b is playing
   c played

9 Extreme Sports

Lesson 1

1 Complete the crossword puzzle.

Across

1 You wear g<u>oggles</u> to protect your eyes.
4 A h_____ keeps you safe from falling.
5 A p_____ carries you through the air.
6 You wear a w_____ in water to keep warm.
7 Your i_____ teaches you how to do sports.

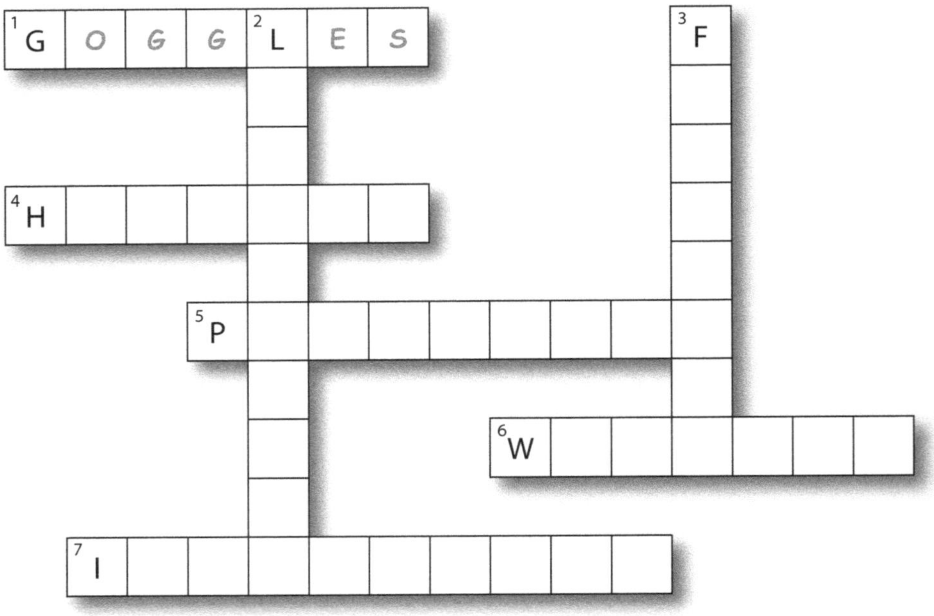

Down

2 You wear a l_____ to keep safe in the water.
3 You wear f_____ to help you swim faster.

2 Circle the correct words.

1 Abseiling was difficult but I got the hang **of** / **with** it in the end.
2 It's important to plan carefully and not take **gloves** / **risks**.
3 When it's very cold, it's easy to **walk** / **slip** on icy roads.
4 Don't **hang** / **lean** too far or you will fall!
5 We can't go to London tonight, it's **simply** / **quickly** too far.

3 Complete the sentences with these words.

> instructors   flippers   gloves   goggles   wetsuit   balcony

1 This _____wetsuit_____ is great for swimming in cold water.
2 _____ help you to swim much faster.
3 Please don't go near the edge of the _____ !
4 It's very important to wear _____ when you're skiing to protect your hands.
5 I usually wear _____ when I'm swimming because I don't like getting water in my eyes.
6 First of all, our _____ showed us the safety equipment.

4 Circle the correct words.

1 If you **won't wear** / **don't wear** gloves when you're abseiling, you burn your hands on the rope.
2 If you wear a wetsuit in the water, your body **is staying** / **stays** warm.
3 If you **go** / **will go** climbing, the instructor will check your harness first.
4 It **is** / **does** easier to abseil down if you lean back.
5 If you **will not be** / **are not** a member, you are not allowed into the extreme sports club.
6 If you **will look down** / **look down** from the top of the building, you will feel really scared.

5 Complete the first conditional sentences with the verbs in brackets.

1 If she ____avoids____ (avoid) eating sweets, she will be healthier.
2 You _____ (get) the hang of it if you practise a bit more.
3 She will get wet if she _____ (go) out cycling in the rain.
4 You _____ (be) safe if you follow my instructions.
5 If the weather is fine tomorrow, I _____ (do) my first ever parachute jump.
6 Unless he _____ (pass) the exam, he can't become an instructor.

6 Write sentences using the first conditional. Then match.

1 if / you / not wear / a helmet / you / may / hurt / your head
   If you don't wear a helmet, you may hurt your head.   [a]

2 I / feel / proud of her / if / she / reach / the bottom of the mountain
   _____   [ ]

3 your hands / get cold / unless / you / wear / warm gloves
   _____   [ ]

4 if / they / wear / their lifejackets / they / be / safe in the raft
   _____   [ ]

5 if / you / not wear / good walking boots / you / may / slip on the rocks
   _____   [ ]

6 unless / he / wear / gloves / he / not be able to / avoid burns from the rope
   _____   [ ]

Lesson 2

1 Match.

1 cliff
2 strength
3 challenge
4 timing
5 score
6 surf

a This is how physically strong you are.
b This is when you ride the waves on a board.
c This is when or how long something is.
d This tells you who is winning.
e You often find this next to the sea. It's tall and rocky.
f This is something difficult that you want to do.

2 Circle the correct words.

1 Diving is an important **tradition** / **tourism** in Acapulco.
2 It's normal to feel **angry** / **fear** when you start diving.
3 The divers dive off the **edge** / **bottom** of a cliff.
4 There are big **waves** / **waters** in the sea in Acapulco.
5 These divers are strong and can deal **with** / **on** the risks.
6 The divers' **aim** / **want** is to win the championship.
7 The Mexican team often **beats** / **wins** the other divers.

3 Complete the sentences with these words.

up   out   up   out   with

1 She started slowly, but then she caught ___up___ with the others and won the race!
2 I dropped _____ of windsurfing last winter because the water was so cold.
3 It's a good idea to warm _____ before you start running.
4 It's hard to deal _____ very strong wind when you are windsurfing.
5 Arif wanted to work _____ this evening but he has too much homework.

64 UNIT 9

4 Complete the second conditional sentences with the verbs in brackets.

1 Katie _____would buy_____ (buy) a horse if she had the money.
2 If she wasn't so scared, she _____ (go) abseiling.
3 He would work out every day if he _____ (have) time.
4 If I _____ (be) you, I wouldn't drop out of the training course.
5 If she knew the dangers, she _____ (not go) skydiving.
6 I _____ (take part) in the race if I had the right equipment.

5 Choose the correct answers.

1 If you _____ Vanuatu, would you go kayaking?
 a visit
 b would visit
 (c) visited

2 We _____ with the others if they slowed down a bit.
 a would catch up
 b caught up
 c will catch up

3 If I were you, I _____ go cycling without a helmet.
 a were
 b didn't
 c wouldn't

4 What would you do if you _____ 18 years old?
 a was
 b were
 c would be

5 If I liked extreme sports, I _____ volcano surfing.
 a would go
 b wouldn't go
 c had to go

6 If you chose to do an extreme sport, which one _____ ?
 a will you do
 b would you do
 c did you do

6 Complete the paragraph with the second conditional. Use the verbs in brackets.

If I (1) ___was / were___ (be) 16 years old, I would go on a kitesurfing course. If there was a kitesurfing centre near my home, I (2) _____ (go) there. I (3) _____ (rent) all my equipment from the kitesurfing centre if I (4) _____ (not have) enough money to buy my own. If I really (5) _____ (enjoy) it, I (6) _____ (save up) the money to buy my own equipment later.

Lesson 3

1 Complete the sentences with these words.

> participant   nickname   chasing   ~~runner~~   tradition   winner

1 A _____runner_____ needs new shoes every six months.
2 Paul's _____ is 'Steam' when he is doing extreme ironing.
3 Do you want to be a _____ in the cheese-rolling race?
4 Extreme ironing is not a _____ in Brockworth.
5 First prize goes to the _____ .
6 The cat was _____ the mouse for an hour!

2 Circle the correct words.

1 If the hill hadn't been so steep, Jerry **(wouldn't have)** / **wouldn't** hurt his foot while running.
2 She **had** / **wouldn't have** hurt her hands if she had worn gloves.
3 If the horse hadn't fallen, it **would** / **will** have won the race.
4 If we **hadn't** / **didn't** missed the train, we would have seen the race.
5 If I hadn't read about the cheese-rolling race on the Internet, I **wasn't** / **wouldn't have** been able to take part in it.
6 If you **ask** / **had asked** me, I would have given you the equipment.

3 Look at the pictures and complete the sentences using adjectives with numbers.

SAY IT LIKE THIS!

1 It's _____a 2-mile_____ walk to Llanwrtyd Wells.
2 There will be _____ break.
3 Ben is _____ boy.
4 He is carrying _____ box.

4 Read the email and replace the formal phrases in bold with these informal phrases. Add capital letters and punctuation as necessary.

> guess what   hi Ben!   how's it going
> let me know   really cool   for ages
> what have you been up to   write soon!

Remember!
We should use informal language in a letter or email to a friend. For example:
How's it going?
What have you been up to?
Let me know …
Guess what?
for ages
… cool …

Email

(1) ~~Dear Mr Jones~~ Hi Ben,

(2) **Are you well**? Did you have a good week at school? We went on a school trip to the National Sports Museum last Wednesday. It was (3) **very enjoyable**.

Everyone in my class went on the trip. We went by bus and the journey took about two hours. I had a snack to eat on the bus and Mum gave me 15 pounds to spend. And (4) **try to imagine**! Dad gave me a new digital camera especially for the trip.

The National Sports Museum displays old and new sports equipment like parachutes, surfboards, bicycles and planes. The best thing was visiting a model of Amelia Earhart's plane! We stayed inside

(5) **for an extremely long time** and pretended to be real pilots. We learnt that when Amelia Earhart was a pilot, flying was considered an extreme sport!

What about you? (6) **What have you been doing lately**? Have you been on any interesting trips recently?

Send me an email and (7) **inform me**.

(8) **Please reply in the near future.**
Steve

---

5 Imagine you went to see an extreme sport on a recent school trip. Write an email to a friend about it. Don't forget to use informal language. Use this plan to help you.

Begin your email like this:
Hi (your friend's name)!

Paragraph 1
Ask your friend one or two questions about him/herself. Mention where you went for the school trip and say when it took place. Say whether you enjoyed the trip.

Paragraph 2
Give details of the journey and say what you took with you on the trip.

Paragraph 3
Describe the place you visited and what you saw and did there. Give details of one thing you really liked and say how long you were there.

Paragraph 4
Ask your friend if he / she has been on any interesting trips. Ask him / her to write to you.

End your email with one of these phrases:
Bye for now! / Write soon!
(your name)

10 Under the Sea

Lesson 1

1 Write the missing letters.

1 This is a place in the sea where fish and turtles live.   c <u>o r a l</u> r <u>e e f</u>

2 This is when the numbers of an animal or plant are small.   e _ _ _ _ _ _ _ _ _

3 Turtles have these to protect them.   s _ _ _ _ _

4 This is where a plant or animal lives.   h _ _ _ _ _ _

5 This word describes the sea.   m _ _ _ _ _

6 This is a kind of machine invented for a special purpose   d _ _ _ _ _

2 Complete the sentences with these words.

> impact   ecosystem   track of   ~~specialises~~   analyse   maintain

1 Bridget is a scientist who __specialises__ in marine biology.

2 We use the device to keep _____ endangered fish.

3 Coral is important for the ocean's _____ .

4 We need to _____ the number of turtles in the world.

5 Pollution has a bad _____ on the habitat of turtles.

6 We will look at the results and _____ them.

3 Match.

1 People kill turtles for their shells.
2 My son is a marine biologist.
3 Fish and turtles need a safe habitat.
4 What is this device used for?
5 How can we have a positive impact on the environment?
6 How can we maintain the numbers of turtles?

a He analyses coral reefs.
b We can avoid polluting marine ecosystems.
c That's why coral reefs are important.
d They are now endangered animals.
e It keeps track of where whales go.
f We must protect their habitats.

4 Complete the sentences with the correct form of the verbs in brackets.

1. I'm sorry I broke the device.
   I wish I _____hadn't_____ broken the device. (have)
2. I didn't specialise in marine biology.
   If only I _____ specialised in marine biology. (have)
3. Carrie throws her rubbish in the sea.
   I wish Carrie _____ her rubbish in the sea. (not throw)
4. I want to see a pink dolphin.
   I wish I _____ a pink dolphin. (can see)
5. They've lost my underwater camera!
   If only they _____ my underwater camera! (not lose)
6. You never listen to me!
   If only you _____ to me! (listen)

5 Complete the sentences with the correct form of the verbs in brackets.

1. I wish I __hadn't taken__ (not take) the wrong boat.
2. I wish she _____ (not have) her pet shark with her.
3. I wish the shark _____ (not chase) me.
4. If only I _____ (not fall) into the sea.
5. I wish the shark _____ (not bite) me!

6 Circle the correct words.

If only I (1) **didn't go / hadn't gone** to the beach yesterday. It was really silly! I was swimming when I thought I saw a massive shark near a small boy. I wish I hadn't (2) **seen / saw** the boy or the thing next to him, now.

I shouted, 'Help! Help!' and I swam back to the beach. I ran up to the lifeguard and I told him I had seen a shark. The lifeguard looked very surprised and said, 'But there aren't any sharks in the sea around here.'

'There must be sharks here because I've just seen one!' I said. 'It's near that boy!'

I wish I (3) **hadn't / didn't** said anything. The lifeguard swam out to the boy to help him. After five minutes he came back to the beach.

'You didn't see a shark. You saw the boy's surfboard!' he laughed. 'You need to wear glasses! I wish you (4) **had / hadn't** looked more carefully.'

If only I hadn't (5) **said / say** anything! I felt stupid and said, 'I'm really sorry. I wish I hadn't (6) **waste / wasted** your time.'

'It's OK,' said the lifeguard. 'You were only trying to help. You know, sometimes I wish there (7) **was / is** a shark here. It's very boring on this beach!'

Lesson 2

1 Choose the correct answers.

1 Port Royal was built inside a _____ .
   (a) fort
   b habitat

2 The ship _____ in the terrible storm.
   a sank
   b fell

3 The ships carried _____ into the harbour.
   a trade
   b goods

4 Archaeologists look for _____ from historical times.
   a artefacts
   b museums

5 _____ stole goods from the Spanish and Dutch ships.
   a Residents
   b Pirates

2 Write the missing letters.

1 This is when you buy and sell goods.   t r a d e
2 Tsunamis and earthquakes are examples of this.   d _ _ _ _ _ _ _
3 This is another word for bad or terrible.   h _ _ _ _ _ _ _
4 This is when you take something without paying for it.   s _ _ _ _
5 This is when someone is taken by force.   c _ _ _ _ _ _
6 This can happen if you do something wrong.   p _ _ _ _ _ _ _ _ _
7 This is a place ships stop in, to take things on and off. h _ _ _ _ _ _

3 Complete the sentences with these words.

| about   by   for   into   with |

1 Did he have an argument ___with___ his mother?
2 There's going to be an investigation _____ the disaster.
3 Tsunamis are often caused _____ earthquakes.
4 The pirates have been captured. There's no doubt _____ it.
5 What is the reason _____ this mess?

70 UNIT 10

4 Match.

1 Nobody helped me.
2 Tina fell off her bicycle.
3 John and I didn't have a nice time.
4 Carl's finger is bleeding.
5 Have a good time!
6 Mum didn't make the boys' beds.

a We didn't enjoy ourselves.
b Enjoy yourself!
c They did it themselves.
d She hurt herself.
e He cut himself.
f I did it by myself.

5 Circle the correct words.

1 Don't walk home by **yourself** / **himself**. It's not safe.
2 He hurt **herself** / **himself** when he fell down.
3 The accident wasn't Maria's fault, but she blames **herself** / **itself** for what happened.
4 Did the men hurt **ourselves** / **themselves**?
5 I keep telling **himself** / **myself** not to get stressed but I can't help it.
6 We are investigating the missing cat **ourselves** / **themselves** because the police aren't helping us.

6 Complete the conversation with reflexive pronouns.

Detective: Mr Finn! Have you hurt (1) _yourself_?

Mr Finn: No, but I'm really fed up. I wish I had caught the pirates! I blame (2) _____ because I should have been more careful.

Detective: Don't worry, we'll catch them. They hurt (3) _____ when they jumped into the sea.

Mr Finn: We always thought (4) _____ safe in this harbour and we don't always remember to lock the cabin door.

Detective: You and your family must remind (5) _____ to lock the cabin door every night in the future.

Mr Finn: You're right! The door won't lock (6) _____ !

Lesson 3

1 Complete the sentences with these words.

> coast   blind   crab   worth   appearance

1 The Kiwa ___crab___ is fluffy and white.

2 Can you see that boat sailing along the _____ ?

3 The treasure was _____ millions of dollars.

4 Clown frogfish can change their _____ to stay safe.

5 Someone who is _____ can't see.

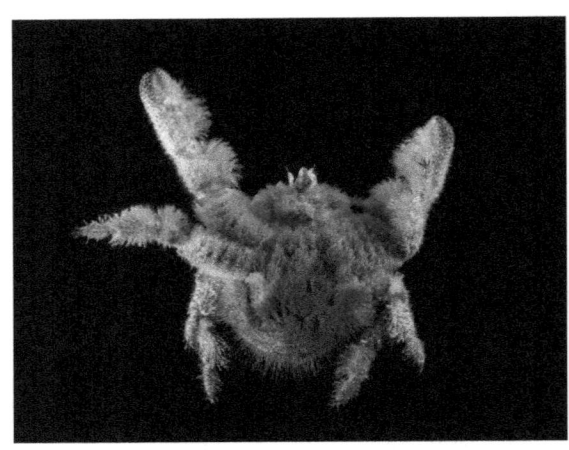

2 Circle the correct words.

SAY IT LIKE THIS!

Ann: Hi Jill!

Jill: Hi Ann! Did you hear (1) **about** / **for** the concert? You won't (2) **believe** / **hear** this! I got two tickets!

Ann: No (3) **matter** / **way**! That's great, Jill but let me tell you…

Jill: Wait! So then I went to the supermarket and lost my wallet!

Ann: Listen to me…

Jill: AND the tickets were inside!

Ann: Well, guess (4) **that** / **what**!

Jill: What?

Ann: I found your wallet!

Jill: You must be (5) **joking** / **looking**! I don't (6) **believe** / **feel** it!

Ann: It's true! Let's go to the concert!

3 Talk to your partner about a natural disaster you have heard about. Explain what happened, where it was and how it was dealt with.

4 Read the story and complete the plan with the correct letters.

Introduction: Paragraph __B__
Middle: Paragraph _____
Paragraph _____
Ending: Paragraph _____

A Anna was right. We had forgotten to tie up the boat and the wind had blown it away from the island. 'What are we going to do?' I said. 'We're all alone on this island! We've eaten all our food. We've got no sleeping bags and no water!'
'You're right,' replied Anna, 'but we have got … my mobile phone!'

B Last summer I was staying at my aunt and uncle's seaside house. The house is situated at the top of a steep rocky cliff. At the bottom is a beautiful sandy beach with wonderful blue water where my cousin, Anna, and I went swimming every day.

C Anna quickly phoned her parents. We had to wait for about two hours but in the end my uncle arrived at the island and rescued us. We were cold and hungry by then. He was pleased to see us, but he was very angry, too! I enjoyed the rest of my holidays but one thing's for sure – I've had enough adventures!

D One day, we decided to take a picnic and sail to a nearby island on my uncle's boat. 'It will be an adventure,' Anna said. We sailed for about an hour and as soon as we reached the island we had our lunch and lay down on the beach for a rest. Suddenly Anna shouted, 'The boat! It's gone!'

Remember!

A good story should have an introduction, a middle and an ending.

5 Write a story that ends with the words 'I've had enough adventures.' Use the questions in the plan to help you.

Paragraph 1: Introduction
Describe the situation.
When did the events in the story take place?
Where is the story set? Describe the setting.
Who are the main characters?

Paragraphs 2 and 3: Middle
Describe the action.
What happened first?
What was the result of that action?
What happened next?
Did something go wrong? If so, what?

Paragraph 4: Ending
Describe how the story ended.
Say how you / the main characters felt.
How do you / they feel about it now?

Review 5 — Units 9–10

1 Read the text about snow leopards.

The snow leopard, which lives in the mountains of central Asia, is among the world's most endangered big cats. Scientists estimate that there may be as few as 3,500 of these animals left in the wild. One of the main reasons for this is that their natural habitat is being destroyed as forests are cut down.

Another reason these animals are endangered is that they are often killed and sold for their fur. They have beautiful coats which can be sold for thousands of dollars. In addition, snow leopard bones and claws are used in traditional Asian medicines and are worth a lot of money.

One of the reasons that local people break the law and kill snow leopards is that they are very poor. Wildlife protection groups which are trying to save the snow leopard believe that it's important to create other jobs for local people so that they won't have to hunt the snow leopard.

Nobody knows exactly what will happen to the snow leopard in the future, but one thing is for sure: wildlife groups will work hard to tell people about these beautiful animals and to try to make sure they continue to live in the wild.

2 Write *R* (Right) or *W* (Wrong) or *DS* (Doesn't Say).

1 The snow leopard lives in Asia. **R**
2 Fewer than 3,500 snow leopards now live in the wild. ☐
3 Snow leopards' fur is used in medicines. ☐
4 Wildlife groups have created new jobs for locals. ☐
5 There will be more snow leopards living in the wild in the future. ☐

3 Choose the correct answers.

1 When I go skiing I wear a hat, gloves and ___ .
   a flippers
   b a lifejacket
   c goggles

2 Archaeologists look for ___ .
   a artefacts
   b harbours
   c pirates

3 This ___ helps us analyse what turtles eat.
   a fear
   b challenge
   c device

4 I play sports to ___ out every day.
   a walk
   b drop
   c work

5 Wear this ___ to stop you from falling.
   a harness
   b wetsuit
   c parachute

6 The athlete's aim is to ___ the others.
   a slip
   b beat
   c risk

7 Jenny dropped ___ the race after she hurt her leg.
   a into
   b up with
   c out of

8 I had an argument ___ Stacy about the money.
   a with
   b to
   c on

9 I still haven't got the ___ of surfing.
   a edge
   b hang
   c slip

10 He ___ 50 dollars from my bag!
   a stole
   b steal
   c catches

11 ___ animals must be protected.
   a Shell
   b Coral
   c Marine

12 Don't ___ over the cliff edge!
   a trade
   b sink
   c lean

4 Choose the correct answers.

1 Mike won't be safe ___ wears a lifejacket.
   a unless he
   b if he
   c unless he doesn't

2 If you ___ , you won't be cold.
   a would dress warmly
   b dress warmly
   c will dress warmly

3 You ___ faster if you wear flippers.
   a swim
   b are swimming
   c swam

4 If he ___ older, he could go rafting with his dad.
   a were
   b is
   c would be

5 If you ___ a helmet, you wouldn't have injured your head.
   a wear
   b do wear
   c had worn

6 If I had enough money, I ___ skydiving lessons.
   a would have
   b had
   c have

7 I wish we ___ the other team in yesterday's match.
   a would beat
   b will beat
   c had beaten

8 ___ I hadn't stolen that money!
   a If only
   b If
   c Unless

9 I wish I ___ strong enough to go climbing!
   a be
   b was
   c am

10 I hope the children will behave ___ at the party.
   a them
   b themselves
   c by themselves

11 I made ___ a delicious sandwich earlier.
   a yourself
   b itself
   c myself

12 Karim wrote this story ___ – isn't he clever?
   a by herself
   b by himself
   c by themselves

75

11 Communication

Lesson 1

1 Match.

1 I'm writing
2 Sally's poem
3 Michael suggested
4 Smiling emojis show
5 In 1881,

a emoticons were first used on purpose.
b is being published in that magazine.
c a text message to my cousin.
d that we communicate by email.
e that you are joking.

2 Complete the sentences with these words.

abbreviation   character   punctuation   ~~symbol~~   type

1 This is the __symbol__ for recycling.
2 The _____ for kilometres is km.
3 A _____ can be a letter or a number.
4 Full stops and commas are both kinds of _____ .
5 Can you _____ without looking at the keyboard?

3 Write the missing letters.

1 This is when you do something because you want to.   o <u>n</u> p <u>u r p o s e</u>
2 This is a way to communicate by mobile phone.   t _ _ _ m _ _ _ _ _ _
3 This is something you say or do to make people laugh.   j _ _ _
4 This is something creative that you write.   p _ _ _
5 This is a shorter way to write a word or phrase.   a _ _ _ _ _ _ _ _ _ _ _
6 This is when you use a keyboard to write.   t _ _ _

76 UNIT 11

4 Complete the sentences.

1 'I'll email her tomorrow,' said Kate.
She said that she __would email__ her tomorrow.

2 'You can use my laptop,' said Beth.
She said that I _____ her laptop.

3 'My brother wrote this poem,' said Sarah.
She said that her brother _____ this poem.

4 'I must get an Internet connection,' said John.
He said that he _____ an Internet connection.

5 'I don't have a mobile phone,' said Steve.
He said that he _____ a mobile phone.

6 'I love using emojis,' said Clare.
She said that she _____ using emojis.

5 Complete the sentences using reported speech.

1 'I'm typing a letter.'
She said that __she was typing a letter__.

2 'You must buy a new computer.'
He said that I _____.

3 'I use the school computer every day.'
She said that _____
_____.

4 'I'll send you an email.'
He said that he _____.

5 'I've never visited that website.'
He said that _____.

6 'We published our photos in a book.'
She said that _____
_____.

6 Read the dialogue and then complete the paragraph using reported speech.

Rebecca: Good morning, I want to buy a laptop.
Assistant: Yes, of course. We have all the new ones right here.
Rebecca: I'm looking for something that's not too expensive.
Assistant: OK, I'll show you this one over here.
Rebecca: Oh, I've seen an advert on TV for this one.
Assistant: Yes, it's a very good laptop.
Rebecca: OK. I'll buy it, please.
Assistant: You must pay for it downstairs. You can take the lift down.
Rebecca: Fine. Thank you.

Rebecca said she (1) __wanted__ to buy a laptop. The assistant told her that they (2) _____ all the new ones. Rebecca said that she (3) _____ for something not too expensive. The assistant said that she (4) _____ her one (5) _____. Rebecca said that she (6) _____ an advert on TV for (7) _____. The assistant said that it was a very good laptop. Rebecca said that she (8) _____ it. The assistant explained that she (9) _____ for it downstairs and that she (10) _____ the lift down.

Lesson 2

1 Circle the odd one out.

1. whistle — (see) — sing
2. complex — simply — easily
3. signal — sign — unique
4. command — tell — suggest
5. identify — express — say
6. research — indicate — investigate

2 Choose the correct answers.

1. Parents feel ____ for their children.
   - (a) affection
   - b command
2. My friend doesn't have a good ____ with her sister.
   - a signal
   - b relationship
3. Some birds can ____ musical instruments.
   - a imitate
   - b whistle
4. Your dog is being ____. Please stop it.
   - a complex
   - b aggressive
5. Every person in the world is ____.
   - a unique
   - b fun

3 Complete the sentences with these words.

> across   off   on   ~~through~~   up

1. I tried to phone Gary, but I couldn't get _through_.
2. I think he made ____ that story about seeing a dolphin.
3. Dad told my baby brother ____ for pulling the cat's tail.
4. I hope we managed to get the message ____ about protecting the dolphin's natural environment.
5. The marine biologist doesn't get ____ very well with her colleagues.

78 UNIT 11

4 Complete the sentences using reported speech.

1
Peter asked Bob
how old he was.

3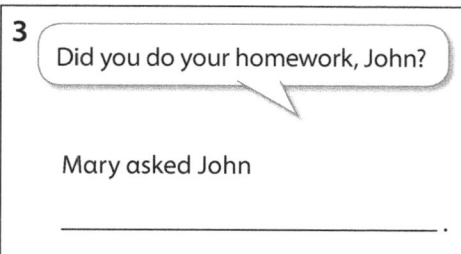
Mary asked John
_____.

5
Steve asked Helen
_____
_____.

2
Jill asked Kate
_____.

4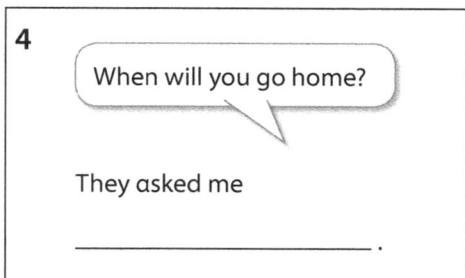
They asked me
_____.

6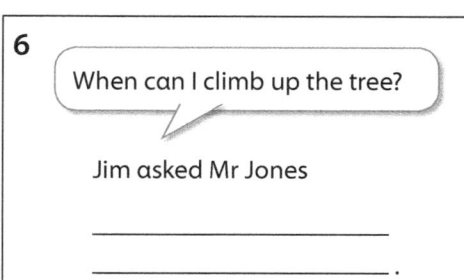
Jim asked Mr Jones
_____
_____.

5 Look at the reported speech and write the direct speech.

1 We asked the marine biologist if the dolphins talked to each other.
   'Do the dolphins talk to each other?'

2 She asked if the scientists had done any experiments.
   _____

3 I asked if she could understand dolphin language.
   _____

4 He asked if the scientists talked over the phone.
   _____

5 He asked if there was any chance that we would understand dolphin language in the future.
   _____

6 Circle the correct words.

1 'Don't speak!' said the man. → The man asked me not **speak** / **(to speak)**
2 'Can you help me?' she asked. → She **asked** / **said** me to help her.
3 'Have any experiments been done?' he asked. → He asked **if** / **have** any experiments had been done.
4 'Don't shout so loudly, Tom!' I said. → I **told** / **said** Tom not to shout so loudly.
5 'Where is the aquarium, please?' he asked. → He asked me to **say** / **tell** him where the aquarium was.
6 'Tell me what happened!' she said. → She **told** / **asked** me to tell her what happened.

Lesson 3

1 **Complete the sentences with these words.**

> meaningful   connection   ~~convenient~~   data   charge   get

1. Sophie says mobile phones are the most ___convenient___ way to communicate.
2. Farrah thinks seeing her friends in person is more _____ .
3. It's hard to make a real _____ with a text message.
4. Ahmed has used all his _____ this month and can't use the Internet.
5. There is no _____ for spending time with friends in person.
6. Jill finds it hard to _____ together with her friends.

2 **Complete the sentences with reported speech.**

1. 'I'm meeting my cousins at the café today,' Amy said.
   Amy said that she ___was meeting___ her cousins at the café ___that day___ .
2. 'My grandmother is taking part in a debate about modern communications tonight,' she said.
   She said that her grandmother _____ in a debate about modern communications _____ .
3. 'I'm going to try to talk to Mum this afternoon,' she said.
   She said that she _____ to try to talk to her mum _____ afternoon.
4. 'I phoned my friend Sarah yesterday and she got the email, too.'
   She said that she _____ her friend Sarah _____ and that she _____ the email, too.
5. 'I chatted with my sister on the phone for four hours last week,' she said.
   She said that she _____ with her sister on the phone for four hours _____ .

3 **Read the sentences about what Carol does. Then complete the sentences about Stuart with *so* or *neither* and the correct form of the verb to show that the same things are also true for Stuart.**

> ### SAY IT LIKE THIS!
>
> 1. Carol uses the Internet to keep in touch with friends. ___So does___ Stuart.
> 2. Carol didn't buy an expensive mobile phone last week. _____ Stuart.
> 3. Carol is doing research for her project the Internet at the moment. _____ Stuart.
> 4. Carol hasn't read this computer magazine yet. _____ Stuart.
> 5. Carol can download photos. _____ Stuart.

4 Read the article and circle the correct phrases.

What are the advantages and disadvantages of using the Internet for school work?

> **Remember!**
>
> We can use these phrases in an article to talk about advantages:
> The good thing about ... is that ...
> What I like about ... is that ...
> One of the main advantages of ... is that ...
> On the one hand, ...
> We can use these phrases in an article to talk about disadvantages:
> On the other hand, ...
> The main problem with ... is that ...
> Another drawback of ... is ...

The Internet is used by many people as a fun way of passing the time. They enjoy surfing the Internet for information or downloading music and photos. In addition, both adults and children use the Internet for work or school.

The (1) **good thing about** / **on the other hand** using the Internet for school work is that you can find out lots of information about any subject. There are thousands of websites with photos, articles and information about maths, physics, geography, music and much more! One of (2) **what I like** / **the main advantages** of using the Internet for school projects is that it's so fast. You don't have to spend hours in the library or reading books in order to find out the information you need.

(3) **Another drawback** / **On the other hand**, students can become lazy by using the Internet. They find a website and simply copy whole paragraphs or articles to use in their projects or homework. This means that they don't really think for themselves or understand the subject properly. (4) **The main problem** / **Another drawback** of using the Internet is that not all the information that you find there is actually true!

In my opinion, students should use the Internet to help them with their school work and to get photos and information, but they shouldn't use *only* the Internet. Books, magazines and TV programmes are also useful and will encourage students to think for themselves.

5 Write an article with the title, 'What are the advantages and disadvantages of using a mobile phone?' Don't forget to use the phrases in the Remember! box. Use this plan to help you.

Paragraph 1
Who uses mobile phones? Why do they use them? How much / often do they use them?

Paragraph 2
Talk about the advantages of using a mobile.

Advantage 1: ...

Advantage 2: ...

Paragraph 3
Talk about the disadvantages of using a mobile.

Disadvantage 1: ...

Disadvantage 2: ...

Paragraph 4
What is your personal opinion?

12 Money

Lesson 1

1 Complete the crossword puzzle.

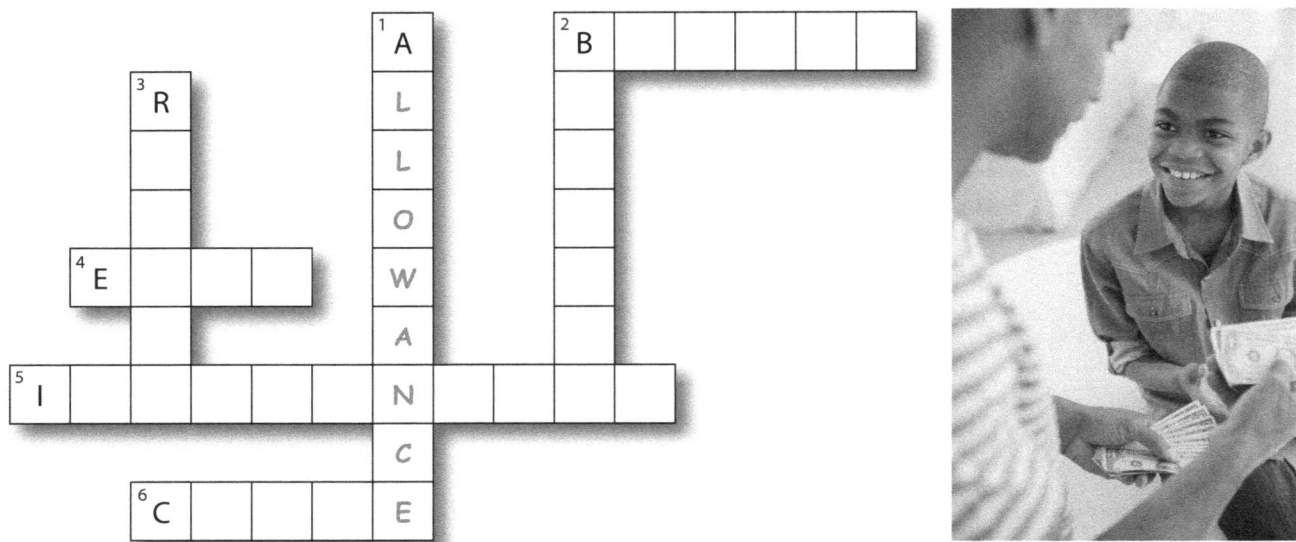

Down

1 Some children get a weekly a**llowance** from their parents.

2 It's a b_____ when you get something for a cheaper price than usual.

3 A r_____ is a kind of prize you get for doing something well.

Across

2 You b_____ to plan how much money you can spend.

4 People e_____ a salary for doing their jobs.

5 An i_____ person doesn't need a lot of help from other people.

6 A c_____ is something boring you have to do.

2 Circle the odd one out.

1 (appreciate)   reward   prize
2 give   hand   receive
3 value   cost   deserve
4 salary   manage   money
5 chore   work   holiday

3 Circle the correct words.

1 My teacher (handed) / told me a pencil because I had forgotten mine.

2 I don't think that Tim **deserves** / **bargains** his high salary. He's so lazy!

3 I **value** / **earn** almost nothing but I'm independent and enjoy my work.

4 It's important to **reward** / **manage** your money carefully.

5 My sister is **working** / **budgeting** for university. She needs to save a lot of money.

82 UNIT 12

4 Complete the sentences with the causative function using the words in brackets.

1 Craig ___had his website designed___ (his website / designed) last year.
2 She _____ (not / milk / deliver) every morning.
3 Next week, he _____ (the house / paint).
4 She _____ (her hair / do) once a week.
5 He _____ (can't / his car / fix) because he doesn't have enough money.

5 Write questions. Use the causative.

1 ? / you / your shoes / clean / every month
   ___Do you have your shoes cleaned every month?___

2 ? / they / a swimming pool / build / next year
   _____

3 ? / you / a dress / deliver / yesterday evening
   _____

4 ? / the children / their photo / take / right now
   _____

5 ? / she / her house / paint / next week
   _____

6 Choose the correct answers.

1 I _____ before nine.
   a must the shop open
   b the shop must have opened
   c must have the shop opened

2 She had the cake _____ at the bakery.
   a made
   b make
   c making

3 Gran _____ once a week.
   a the shopping delivers
   b has the shopping delivered
   c has delivered the shopping

4 Mr Jones _____ his glasses fixed today.
   a isn't having
   b hasn't
   c haven't

5 _____ the books delivered?
   a Will be
   b Will you deliver
   c Will you have

Lesson 2

1 Match.

1 credit card — e
2 wheat — ☐
3 coin — ☐
4 currency — ☐
5 cattle — ☐
6 note — ☐

a
b (wheat)
c (coins)
d (notes)
e
f

2 Complete the sentences with these words.

> exchange   extra   international
> standard   cash   ~~access~~

1 Cashpoints make it easier for people to _____access_____ their money.

2 People _____ goods in bartering systems.

3 Very little of the world's currency is physical _____ . Most money is digital.

4 If you have more of something than you need, you have _____ .

5 A _____ currency allows _____ trade to happen more easily.

3 Choose the correct answers.

1 These trainers are _____ special offer. Shall we buy them?
 a in
 (b) on
 c at

2 I think that pink flowery hat will go _____ fashion really quickly.
 a in to
 b up to
 c out of

3 I wonder if they have this dress _____ my size?
 a in
 b for
 c on

4 These shoes are beautiful! I hope they don't cost _____ 100 pounds.
 a in
 b over
 c up

5 Excuse me, are these earrings here _____ sale?
 a at
 b in
 c for

84 UNIT 12

4 Complete the sentences with *in order to* or *so that*.

1 She's saving up all her money ___in order to___ buy a pair of designer jeans.
2 Mum is going to get some cash _____ she can pay for the window cleaner.
3 Astronauts wear moon boots _____ they can walk in space.
4 He paid with his credit card _____ impress his friends.
5 Andy went into town _____ exchange some currency.

5 Complete the second sentence so that it means the same as the first. Use the words in bold.

1 These shoes are very comfortable, but they're quite expensive. **although**
___Although these shoes are very___ comfortable, they're quite expensive.

2 It was raining, but we went hiking. **despite**
_____ , we went hiking.

3 Although she didn't like the shells, she decided to buy them. **fact**
She decided to buy the shells, in _____ that she didn't like them.

4 She paid by credit card even though the book cost one dollar. **fact**
Despite _____ , she paid by credit card.

5 Despite not having any money, Steve spent hours in the supermarket. **although**
Steve spent hours in the supermarket _____ any money.

6 Complete the paragraph with these words.

(despite   ~~although~~   in order to   in spite   so that)

(1) ___Although___ we now think of money as notes and coins, many countries used to use shells as cash. The shell used was the 'cowrie' shell. It's a small, white shell that is found in the Pacific and Indian oceans.

Cowrie shells were an important international currency used (2) _____ trade across the world. The shells were often made into jewellery (3) _____ they were easier to carry.

(4) _____ the appearance of metal coins in the 12th century, cowrie shells were used as money into the 20th century. They were so important in China that (5) _____ of not being used today, the character for cowrie - 貝 - is still seen in many Chinese phrases about money.

Lesson 3

1 Circle the correct words.

1 People often advertise activities and concerts on local **noticeboards** / **windows**.

2 Do you want to come over later? I'm **hosting** / **eating** a games night.

3 Sam is going to **sell** / **volunteer** at his local animal shelter tomorrow.

4 It's a beautiful night. Let's go star-**looking** / **gazing**!

5 There's a football **tournament** / **prize** at school this weekend. Are you playing?

2 Complete the dialogue with these words.

> let's   instead   maybe   ~~got~~   would   meet   sounds

Jane: Hi Ben. Listen, I've (1) ___got___ an idea!

Ben: Hi Jane. Cool – what is it?

Jane: (2) _____ go to the beach this afternoon and learn to windsurf.

Ben: It's a great idea, but there's a problem. It's not windy today.

Jane: You're right. It's not windy at all! (3) _____ we could do something else (4) _____?

Ben: Yes. (5) _____ you like to learn to dive?

Jane: Yes, that (6) _____ fun.

Ben: Brilliant. There's a diving instructor at the beach this afternoon. Let's (7) _____ there at two o'clock.

Jane: Great! See you there.

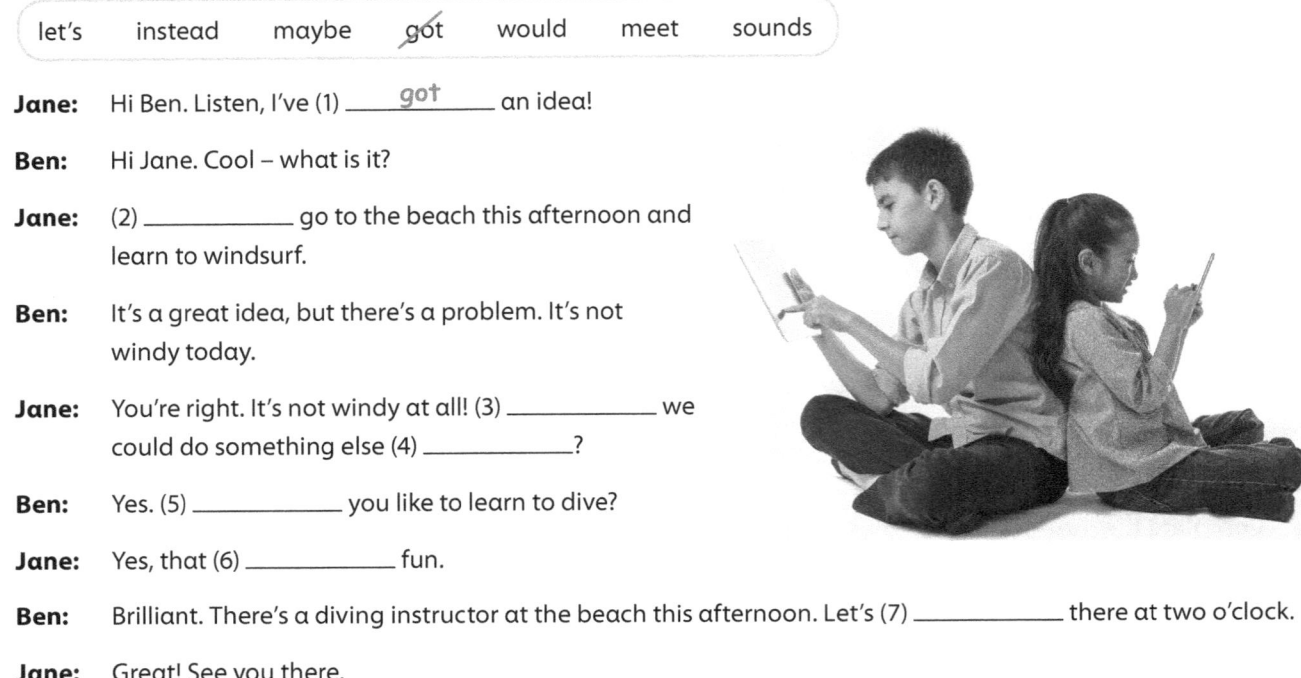

3 Work with a partner. Imagine you're planning a day out with a friend. Use the information and the phrases from Activity 2 to make a dialogue.

> Maybe we could …

> Would you like to go to the …

4 Read the report and choose suitable headings for the main paragraphs. Be careful, there are two headings you don't need.

Advantages   ~~Aim~~   Conclusion
Drawbacks   Existing shopping facilities
Local businesses   The new shopping mall

A New Shopping Mall: Do we need it?

(1) _____ Aim _____

The purpose of this report is to discuss whether a new shopping mall should be built in Amberley.

(2) _____

The council has been asked for permission to build a new shopping mall on the edge of the town which will include three floors of shops as well as a cinema, a restaurant and an Internet café.

(3) _____

Many people in Amberley often drive to London in order to do their shopping because they feel that our small town cannot provide the variety of products and the bargains which are available in the city. The new shopping mall would offer the choice that they require. In addition, it would provide 60 jobs for local people.

(4) _____

However, many of our small businesses, including food stores, gift shops and boutiques rely on local people to support them. If the shopping mall is built, many customers will stop shopping in Amberley town centre. The large building would also ruin the beauty of the landscape on the edge of the town.

(5) _____

Although the new shopping mall would offer many advantages to customers in the area, it has some serious drawbacks. We should think carefully about the needs of local businesspeople before deciding to build a shopping mall which could cause an important change in our way of life here in Amberley.

> **Remember!**
> A report includes several paragraphs, each of which has a heading. In the first paragraph you should state the aim of the report and in the last paragraph you should give a conclusion.

5 Write a report with the title, 'New Sports and Leisure Centre: do we need it?' Give each of your main paragraphs a heading. Use this plan to help you. Add notes of your own to the plan.

Aim
Briefly describe the purpose of your report.

Paragraph 1: Description
Describe the new sports and leisure centre. Where will it be located? What facilities will it offer (pool, tennis, gym, café, Internet access, etc)?

Paragraph 2: Advantages
Talk about the advantages of the new sports and leisure centre.
Advantage 1: ...
Advantage 2: ...

Paragraph 3: Drawbacks
Talk about the drawbacks of the new sports and leisure centre.
Drawback 1: ...
Drawback 2: ...

Conclusion
Give your conclusion in favour of or against the centre, or explain that further research is necessary.

Review 6 — Units 11–12

1 Read the text about communication.

People began to communicate over long distances in the 1830s. That was when the first telegraph machines* were built. Samuel Morse developed the communication system called the Morse code. Messages were sent from one location to another using electricity.

The telephone was then invented in 1876 by Alexander Graham Bell. The telephone was like the telegraph but used electricity to send sound over distances. People slowly began to put telephones into their homes and offices. Almost everyone has a telephone now and most people also have mobile phones.

The mobile phone was invented in 1973 by Martin Cooper. A mobile phone sends your voice over the air to a nearby tower. The tower then sends your voice to the person you are calling. Mobile phones work well when they are near towers, but not so well if they are far away from a tower.

There are many ways to communicate today, including sending text messages and emails. Who knows how we'll be communicating in the future?

*machines that send messages over long distances

2 Answer the questions.

1. When were the first telegraph machines built?   _in the 1830s_
2. What is Morse code?   _____
3. What was invented in 1876?   _____
4. Who invented the mobile phone?   _____
5. When do mobile phones work well?   _____

3 Choose the correct words.

1 His book was ___ last month.
   a published
   b texted
   c communicated

2 Some animals are ___ when scared.
   a unique
   b aggressive
   c imitated

3 The ___ of centimetres is cm.
   a command
   b affection
   c abbreviation

4 Writing poems helps me to ___ myself.
   a express
   b message
   c receive

5 I have a great ___ with my parents.
   a relationship
   b complex
   c purpose

6 Do your parents give you an ___ each week?
   a bargain
   b credit card
   c allowance

7 These trousers are so ___ fashion now!
   a in to
   b out of
   c over

8 I have lots of ___ to do before I go out tonight.
   a chores
   b budgets
   c rewards

9 Sarah made ___ a story about her job.
   a on
   b up
   c in

10 I'm going to send this ___ message to my grandma.
   a letter
   b song
   c text

11 I got three for the price of one; what a great ___!
   a bargain
   b pleasure
   c variety

12 The boat sank. It was a ___.
   a disaster
   b horrible
   c whistle

4 Choose the correct words.

1 I told him ___ my laptop.
   a to do damage
   b not to damage
   c not damage

2 She ___ she would be late.
   a tell me
   b told
   c told me

3 They said they ___ me a new mobile.
   a would buy
   b will have bought
   c did buy

4 She asked if I ___ made for the wedding.
   a was having a new dress
   b have a new dress
   c was making a new dress

5 Zoe said that she had bought the cat the day ___.
   a next
   b then
   c before

6 Dan asked me ___ that afternoon.
   a what I was doing
   b what was I doing
   c what am I doing

7 She told me not to speak at ___ moment.
   a this
   b that
   c those

8 ___ your shopping delivered to the house?
   a Do you have
   b Are they
   c Have

9 She wore her new shoes to work ___ to look smart.
   a for
   b in order
   c so

10 ___ his messy appearance, he got the job!
   a Despite
   b In spite
   c Although

11 In spite of ___ very rich, he drives an old car.
   a to be
   b being
   c be

12 Although ___ those trainers, they're too expensive for me to buy.
   a liking
   b I will like
   c I like

PROJECT 1
Fascinating Places

1 Write the names of the things you need on a trip into the desert.

1. walking boots

3. _____

4. _____

2. _____

2 Match the names of the places with the descriptions.

1. waterfall
2. canyon
3. bridge
4. ancient monument
5. border
6. desert

a. The place where one country meets another country.
b. The place where a river goes over a cliff and the water drops down so that it can continue below.
c. A very old building or statue.
d. The place where a river has cut through mountains to make a deep gorge.
e. Something that is built over a river so you can cross it.
f. A region that receives very little rainfall, not enough to support most plants.

3 Work in pairs. Plan a one-week trip around your country. You will need to:

- find a map of your country
- start and finish in the place where you live
- decide where you want to go and what you want to see and do there (remember you only have seven days)
- decide how you will travel (if you want to use public transport, find out when buses, planes, boats and trains depart and how long the journeys take)
- make a list of things to take

Use the grid below to make your plans.

Day	From (place and time)	To (place and time)	Transport (length of journey)	Activity	Things to take
Monday	Alexandria (06:00)	Cairo (09:00)	Bus: 3 hours	Visit museum	Money, guidebook
1					
2					
3					
4					
5					
6					
7					

4 Draw a big map showing the planned route of your trip.

Write the names of the places and the things you will see and do at each place. Draw lines between the places and write the length of time each journey will take.

5 Bring your map and plan to school. With your partner, give a short talk about your planned trip. Remember to:

- speak clearly and slowly
- show each part of your trip on the map
- take it in turns to speak about each day
- ask your classmates if they have any questions at the end

6 Write a description of 100–200 words about your trip.

PROJECT 2

Science and Technology

1 Look at the pictures and label them. Write the year you think each one was invented.

> space rocket   television   wheel   watch   ~~camera~~   car

camera 1860

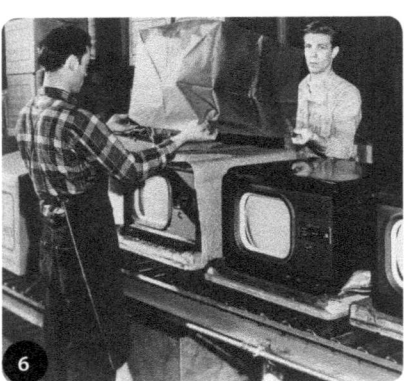

2 What do modern versions of the objects in Activity 1 look like? Make some notes on how they would be different from these pictures.

Compare your ideas with a partner.

	Activity 1 picture	Modern version
1 camera	heavy	small, light, easy to use …
2 television		
3 wheel		
4 watch		
5 space rocket		
6 car		

92   PROJECT 2

3 Choose one object and research its invention. Make some notes about it.

- What is the invention? Describe it. _____
- Who invented it? _____
- Where and when did they invent it? _____
- How has it changed over time? _____
- How old is your object? _____
- Other information … _____

4 Write a 100-word paragraph about your object. Use your notes from Activity 3.

5 Make a poster using your writing and pictures.

6 Bring your poster to school and display it. Look at the other posters. Whose is the most interesting?

DVD players have replaced video.

Many people still have a traditional phone at home.

PROJECT 3
Natural Wonders

1 Look at the pictures and label them.

> palaeontologist   fossil   bones   dinosaur

1. fossil

3. _____

2. _____

4. _____

2 Write some sentences explaining what a palaeontologist does. Do you think it is an interesting job?

A palaeontologist is a scientist who studies fossils of animals and plants...

3 Work in pairs. Choose one dinosaur (for example: Tyrannosaurus Rex, Apatosaurus, Triceratops) and research it. Make some notes about it.

- name _____
- when it lived _____
- where it lived _____
- what it ate _____
- size, shape, colour _____
- other information _____

4 Draw and colour a large picture or make a model of your dinosaur.

5 Write up your notes from Activity 3 as complete sentences. Put each fact on a separate piece of paper, then stick them around your dinosaur picture / model.

6 Bring your dinosaur project to school and display it. Look at your classmates' work. Whose is the best?

7 Write up your dinosaur information as a complete paragraph.

Legends and Folktales

1 Look at the six pictures. They tell a story. Write what happened beneath each picture.

1. The hat seller sat under a tree. He was very tired and …

2 Compare your version of the story with a partner's story. Is it the same or different?

3 Work in groups of four. Invent a story which has four characters. Your story must have six main events. Make notes about what happens on the grid below.

First,	
Then,	
After that,	
Next,	
Then,	
Finally,	

4 Decide how to act out your story, and who is going to tell each of the six events.

5 Practise your story a few times.

6 Perform your story for the other groups and watch theirs. Whose was the best? Which was the funniest?

PROJECT 5
Ambitions

1 Look at the pictures and label them. Decide how difficult you think the jobs are, and why. In the boxes, write a number from 1–10. 1 is very easy and 10 is very difficult.

> lorry driver   teacher   ~~firefighter~~   musician   doctor   footballer

1. firefighter

3. _____

5. _____

2. _____

4. _____

6. _____

2 Work in pairs. Compare your results and say why you think the jobs are more or less difficult.

3 Choose one job which you think is very difficult and research it. Make some notes about your job.

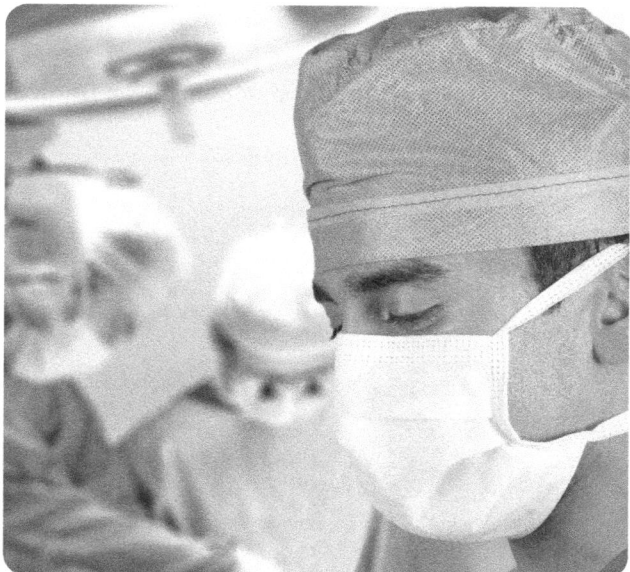

a surgeon

a kindergarten teacher

- qualifications needed   _____
- hours a day worked   _____
- holidays each year   _____
- what you do each day   _____
- why you think it's difficult _____
- salary   _____
- other information   _____

4 Find or draw a picture of someone doing the job you have chosen.

5 Write a paragraph of 75–100 words about your chosen job. Use your notes from Activity 3. What makes the job so difficult?

6 Bring your writing and picture to school. Work in groups of four. Read the others' writing and look at their pictures. Decide which job is the most difficult and why.

PROJECT 6

Remarkable People

1 Look at the pictures and write the correct year next to these four facts about paralympian Karen Darke.

1. __1992__ After becoming paralysed after a running accident, she started hand cycling
2. _____ Won a silver medal in a road time trial in the London Olympic Games
3. _____ Won a gold medal (and a doll) in a road time trial in the Rio Olympic Games
4. _____ Received an MBE from the Queen

2012

1992

2016

2017

2 Complete this biography of Karen Darke using the dates and information in Activity 1.

_____
_____
_____
_____
_____
_____

3 Work in pairs. Compare your biography with your partner's and check that you have the same information in the same order.

4 Choose someone to write a biography about. It can be someone famous or someone that you know. Make notes about the person's life.

- where / when was he / she born? _____
- education _____
- what he / she does _____
- if he / she is famous, why _____
- important dates and events in his / her life _____
- other information _____

5 Find or draw a picture of your chosen person.

6 Write some sentences about your person's life. Use the example biography in Activity 1 and your notes in Activity 4 to help you.

For example: _____

7 Bring your biography and picture(s) to school and make a display. Look at your classmates' work.

8 Write out your person's biography as a paragraph.

PROJECT 7 Body and Mind

1 Look at the pictures and decide if they are healthy or unhealthy.

unhealthy

2 Work in pairs. Compare your answers with your partner's. Do you agree about what is healthy and unhealthy?

3 Use the pictures to write four sentences about what you *should* and *shouldn't* do to be healthy.

1 You shouldn't watch too much TV because it isn't healthy. You should…

2 _____

3 _____

4 _____

4 Make a list of four common health problem.

1. The common cold
2. _____
3. _____
4. _____

5 Choose one of the health problems and research some traditional remedies. Ask your parents or grandparents to help you. Make some notes about the remedies. Do people still use them today? If not, what do people do instead?

6 Draw some pictures of the remedies and label them. Prepare to tell the class about them.

7 Bring your notes and pictures to school. Give a short talk to the class. Talk about your health problem, traditional remedies and modern alternatives.

I'm going to tell you about traditional remedies for the common cold. You can put...

PROJECT 8 The Arts

1 Look at the pictures and label them.

> singing   traditional dancing   weaving   calligraphy   sculpture   ~~drama~~

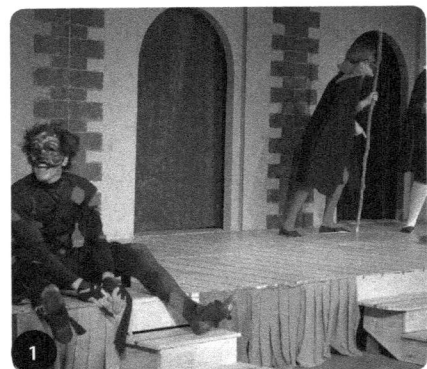
1. drama

3. _____

5. _____

2. _____

4. _____

6. _____

2 Work in pairs. Check your answers with your partner. Have you got the same answers?

3 Which of these art forms can you find in your country? Are there any other traditional arts? Make a list.

_____
_____
_____
_____

4 Work in pairs. Ask and answer these questions.

1 Which of the six arts in Activity 1 do you like? Why?

I like traditional dancing because I think it's …

2 Which of them don't you like? Why?

3 Which of these arts have you seen? When? Where?

5 Choose one art from your culture and research it. Make some notes about it.
- When did it start?
- What does it involve?
- Where can you see it?
- Are there any famous artists?
- Are there any similar arts?
- How is this one different?
- Other information

6 Find or draw some pictures about your chosen art.

7 Write a paragraph about your chosen art. Use your notes from Activity 5.

8 Make a poster using your writing and pictures.

9 Bring your poster to school and display it. Look at your classmates' posters. Which art is the most popular? Which poster is the most interesting?

PROJECT 9

Extreme Sports

1 **Look at the pictures and label them.**

> blobbing   unicycle hockey   ~~elephant polo~~   zorb balling

elephant polo

2 **Answer the questions.**

1 If you had to do one of these four sports, which one would you choose? Why?

2 Which of the four sports do you think is the strangest? Why?

_____
_____
_____
_____
_____
_____

3 **Work in pairs. Invent a strange sport of your own. Make some notes about it and prepare to give a short talk.**
- What is it called? _____
- Which other sport(s) is it like? _____
- What equipment do you need? _____
- How many players are there? _____
- Are there teams? _____
- How do you win? _____
- What are the rules? _____
- Where do you play it? _____
- Other information _____

4 **With your partner, draw and colour some pictures of the pitch, equipment and people playing your sport.**

5 **Write a description of your sport. Use your notes from Activity 3.**

_____
_____
_____
_____
_____
_____
_____
_____

6 **Bring your pictures and description to school. With your partner, give a short talk on your sport. Listen to the other talks. Which sport is the strangest?**

We're going to talk about a strange sport called…. You play it in…. There are four players in each team… .

PROJECT 10 Under the Sea

1 Look at the pictures and label them.

> seahorse   nautilus   whale shark   ~~brain coral~~

brain coral

2 What features do the sea creatures have? Look and write *Y* (Yes), *N* (No) or *DN* (Don't Know).

	can swim	has fins to help it swim	has a shell to protect it	has scales	eats plankton (a very small animal)
seahorse	Y				
brain coral					
nautilus					
whale shark					

3 Work in pairs. Check your answers with your partner. Have you got the same answers?

4 **Work in pairs. Ask and answer these questions.**

1 Which of the sea creatures in Activity 1 do you think is the most unusual? Why?
I think the nautilus is the most unusual because it's …

2 Which of the sea creatures in Activity 1 do you think is the most interesting? Why?

3 Which of the sea creatures in Activity 1 do you think is the most beautiful? Why?

5 **Work in pairs. Choose a sea creature and research it. Make some notes about it.**
- name
- where it lives
- what it eats
- size, shape, colour
- other features
- interesting fact

6 **Draw and colour a large picture or make a model of your sea creature.**

7 **Write up your notes from Activity 5 as complete sentences. Put each fact on a separate piece of paper, then stick them around your sea creature picture / model.**

8 **Bring your sea creature project to school and display it. Look at your classmates' work. Whose is the best?**

9 **Write up your sea creature information as a complete paragraph.**

PROJECT 11
Communication

1 Look at the pictures and label them.

> mobile phone   radio   letter   email

letter

_____

_____

_____

2 Work in pairs. Check your answers with your partner. Which of these communication systems do you use most often?

_____

3 Find out how a mobile phone works. Write some sentences about it.

_____

_____

_____

_____

_____

110   PROJECT 11

4 Work in pairs. Choose one of these communication systems.

flag signalling

Morse code

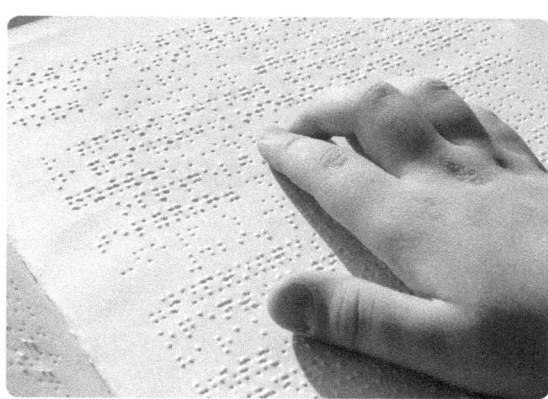

Braille

hieroglyphics

Do some research and make some notes about it and prepare to give a talk.

- Who invented it?   _____
- When was it invented?   _____
- In what situations is it used?   _____
- Is it still used today?   _____
- What are its advantages and disadvantages?   _____
- Other information

5 Find or draw examples of the code your system uses.

6 Write a description of 75–100 words about your chosen system. Use your notes from Activity 4.

7 Bring your writing and pictures to school. Give a talk about your system to the class.
Listen to the other talks. Compare the systems as a class.

PROJECT 12 Money

1 Look at the pictures and label them.

~~bookshop~~ bakery toyshop electrical shop

1. bookshop

3. _____

2. _____

4. _____

2 Work in pairs. Check your answers with your partner. Take it in turns to say where the nearest of each of these shops is to your school.

3 Choose two of the shops. Write some sentences about each of your favourite shops. Say where it is and why you think it's the best.

My favourite bookshop is Green's on the corner of Park Street and Bridge Street. I like it best because …

4 Imagine you have your own shop. Make some notes about it.

- What sort of shop is it? _____
- What is it called? _____
- What does it sell? _____
- How big is it? _____
- How many people work there? _____
- When is it open? _____
- Where is it located? _____
- Other information _____

5 Draw pictures of the inside of your shop and your shop window. Make a floorplan.

6 Write a description of your shop. Use your notes from Activity 4.

7 Make a poster using your writing and pictures, or make a model of your shop.

8 Bring your poster / model to school and display it. Look at your classmates' work. Whose shop looks the best? Whose shop looks the most interesting?

Crossword Puzzles

Units 1–2

Complete the crossword puzzle.

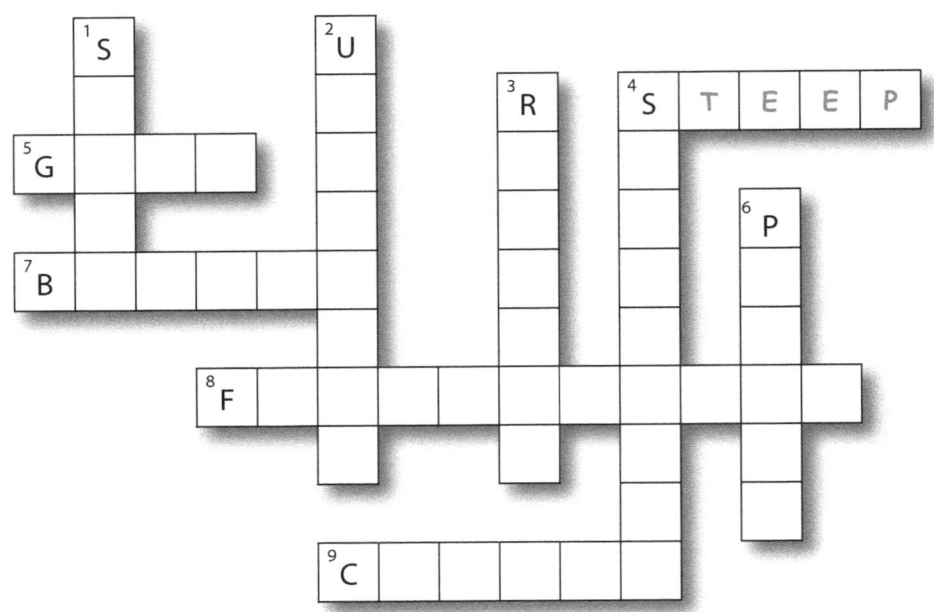

Across

4 The hill was very ____steep____ and hard to climb.

5 The stars _____ in the sky at night.

7 They've built a new _____ across the river.

8 I'm really interested in biology. It's _____ .

9 My parents are artistic. They _____ beautiful paintings.

Down

1 There are nine planets in our _____ system.

2 The _____ is full of stars, planets and galaxies.

3 Elspeth loves _____ down big rivers. It's her favourite sport.

4 There's an interesting _____ by a famous artist in this park.

6 Scientists think there might be alien life on the _____ Mars.

Units 3–4

Complete the crossword puzzle.

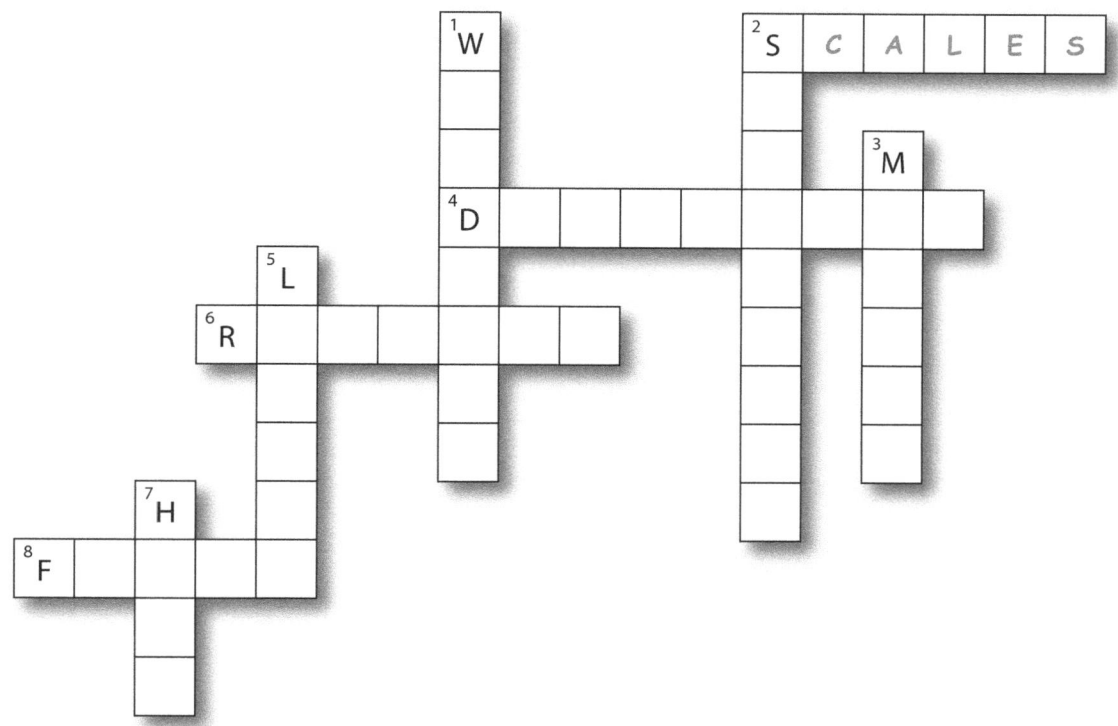

Across

2 Most fish have ____scales____ on their bodies.

4 Boats often _____ in the Bermuda Triangle.

6 A snake is a _____ that doesn't have legs.

8 When it rains too much there can sometimes be a _____.

Down

1 The _____ burnt all the trees and plants in the nature reserve.

2 A _____ happens when a storm damages a boat at sea.

3 A duck-billed platypus is a _____ that lays eggs.

5 My favourite _____ is about the Yeti in Nepal.

7 The rhinoceros is an animal with one _____.

Units 5–6

Complete the crossword puzzle.

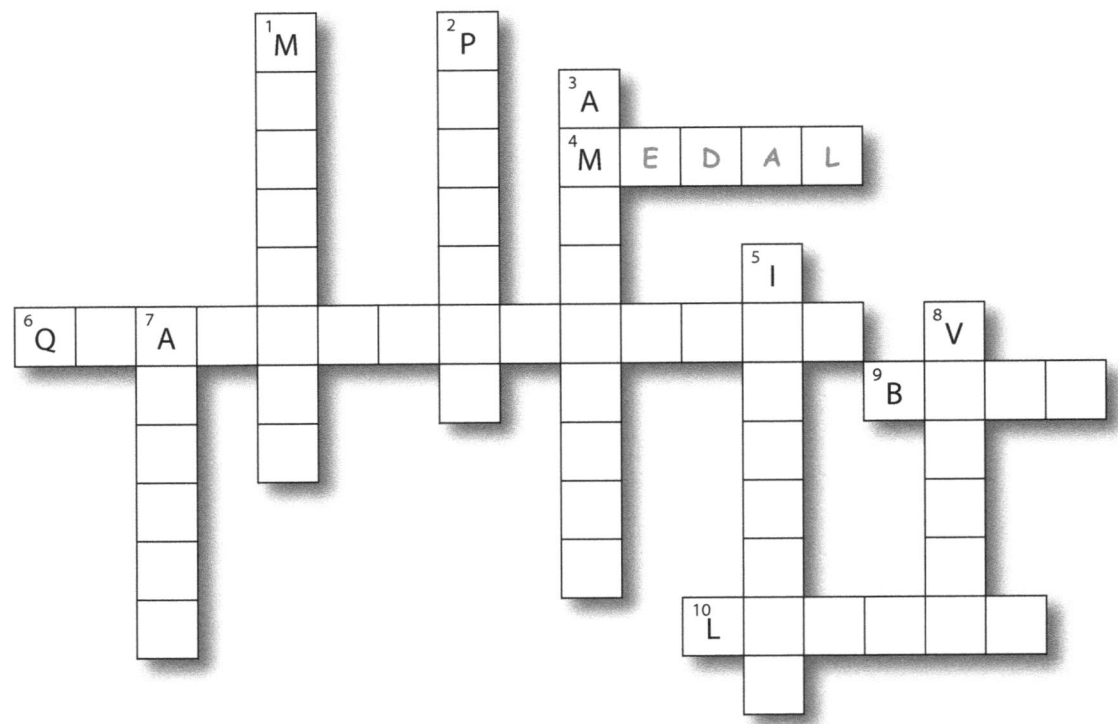

Across

4 The athlete has won a gold ___medal___ in the race.

6 Sarah has lots of _____, but she hasn't got a job.

9 My _____ offered me a higher salary yesterday.

10 Every politician needs to be a good _____.

Down

1 Mika is a talented _____. He taught himself to play the violin.

2 I'm starting a new research _____ today. Can you help me?

3 Nazan is an _____ woman. She works really hard and has lots of goals.

5 My friend Yan really _____ me. She is a famous lawyer.

7 Can you give me some _____? I don't know which career to choose.

8 Amelia Earhart disappeared on her _____ to Howland Island.

Complete the crossword puzzle.

Across

1 Asma is in a very good _____mood_____ today!

5 Sam _____ with his rock band every Saturday.

8 Are you feeling _____? Let's go for a run!

10 The weather is _____ today. I don't think we can go hiking.

Down

2 Would you like to _____ some money to help sick elephants?

3 If your leg is really _____, you need to go to the doctor.

4 I'm _____ after playing tennis. I'm going to bed now.

6 I think Tomas is very _____ because his exams start next week.

7 You really hurt my _____ when you said I was stupid.

9 The new local _____ centre is really cool and modern.

Complete the crossword puzzle.

Across

2 I'm sorry I can't come to your party. The ____timing____ is bad for me.

4 You can't _____ if there aren't any waves.

5 I need some new _____ to keep my hands warm.

7 Coral reefs provide an _____ which we must maintain.

9 People who _____ turtle shells are having a negative impact on numbers.

10 My driving _____ said I was ready to take the test.

Down

1 I enjoy climbing because I don't take any _____ .

3 If you wear _____ when you swim, you can see more fish.

6 George is going to _____ in marine biology at university.

8 My arm is broken because I _____ on the ice and fell.

Units 11–12

Complete the crossword puzzle.

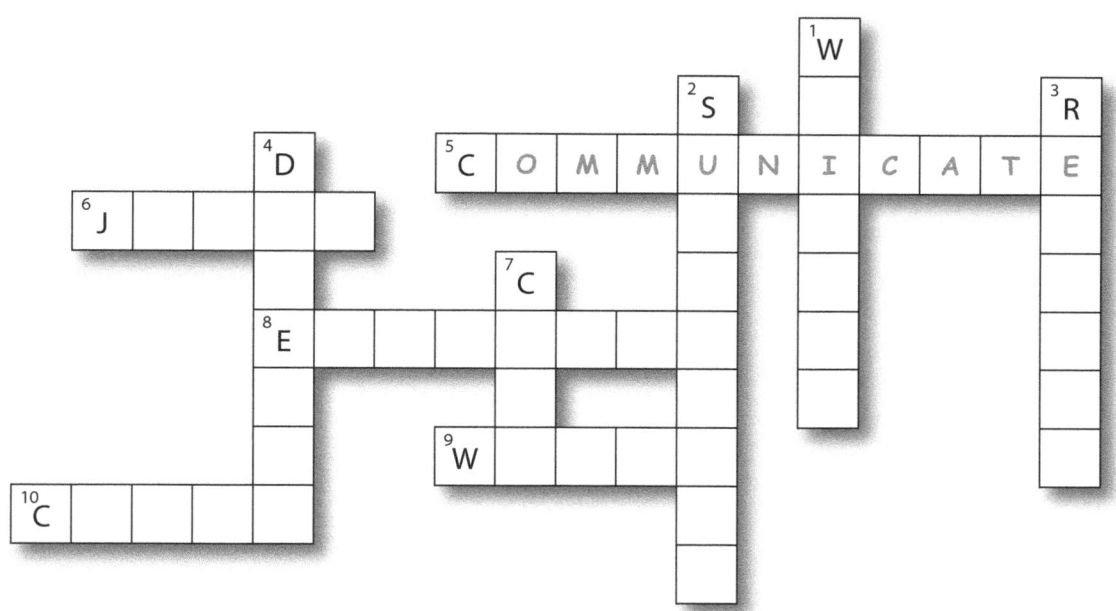

Across

5 I usually __communicate__ with my friends by text message.

6 Where did you learn to tell such funny _____?

8 This shirt is too big. Can I _____ it for one in my size, please?

9 Bread is often made from _____.

10 Washing up is a _____ that I really don't enjoy doing.

Down

1 Can you _____ my favourite tune, please?

2 He _____ going swimming but I wanted to play football.

3 Do you _____ an allowance from your parents?

4 They _____ a medal for working so hard!

7 Your credit card isn't working. Can you pay by _____?

Photo Credits

23 Aleksandar-pal Sakala/Dreamstime; **72(t)** David Shale/NPL/Minden; **98(bm)** Flexograf/Dreamstime; **112(tl)** PL.TH/Fotolia

© Alamy Stock Photo: **22(l)** Glenn Bartley/All Canada Photos; **35(t)** INSADCO Photography; **64(t)** David Bal; **69** G&M Therin-Weise/Robertharding; **84(tm)** www.BibleLandPictures.com; **88** Patrik Argast; **92(br)** Everett Collection Historical; **100(tl)** PA Images; **100(bl)** PA Images; **100(br)** PA Images; **106(tr)** Sasa Huzjak

© Getty Images: **7** Elisalocci/iStock; **14(tl)** QAI Publishing/Universal Images Group; **14(tm)** PhotoDisc; **14(tr)** PhotoDisc; **18** Stephen Alvarez/National Geographic; **21(b)** Ig0rZh/iStock; **50** Hero Images; **59** Roberto Machado Noa/LightRocket; **74** Steve Winter/National Geographic; **92(tm)** Portland Press Herald; **94(tr)** Tim Boyle; **100(tr)** Christopher Lee; **104(tr)** Howard Sochurek/The LIFE Picture Collection; **106(br)** GARI GARAIALDE/AFP

© iStockphoto: **12(b)** Gelpi; **25(b)** Ssuaphoto; **29** CoreyFord; **38(t)** Frentusha; **49(t)** Jennyhorne; **49(f)** Shironosov; **98(tm)** Jacob Wackerhausen; **98(bl)** Ivz; **110(bl)** Tsidvintsev

© Shutterstock: **4(tl)** Monkey Business Images; **4(tm)** Mypokcik; **4(tr)** Strelka; **4(bl)** 3445128471; **4(br)** Taedong; **6(tl)** Dibrova; **6(bl)** Shanty Pictures; **6(tm)** Joyfull; **6(bm)** Renata Sedmakova; **6(tr)** Checubus; **6(b)** Chuckstock; **8(tl)** CEW; **8(bl)** Ron Hilton; **8(tm)** Janne Hamalainen; **8(bm)** Galyna Andrushko; **8(tr)** Air Images; **9** MANDY GODBEHEAR; **10(tr)** Rodho; **10(m)** AridOcean; **11(t)** David Hughes; **11(b)** Alexander Chaikin; **12(tl)** Fotocrisis; **12(bl)** Happy Stock Photo; **12(tm)** Graeme Dawes; **12(bm)** Mariya Pyryeva; **12(tr)** Arunas Gabalis; **12(br)** Bogdan Ionescu; **13** Shcherbakov Ilya; **14(bl)** BestStockFoto; **14(bm)** Naeblys; **14(br)** Ollyy; **15(t)** SergeyDV; **15(b)** Jurgen Ziewe; **16** Wision; **17(t)** Luminis; **17(b)** Alexander Kolomietz; **20** Petrov Stanislav; **21(t)** Ivonne Wierink; **22(m)** PetlinDmitry; **22(r)** 3drenderings; **24(r)** ESB Professional; **24(l)** Observe.co; **25(t)** Tobkatrina; **27** Sculpies; **30** Dibrova; **31(tl)** Yoko Design; **31(tm)** Kak2s; **31(mr)** Yoko Design; **31(b)** Katrien1; **32** Pi-Lens; **34(t)** Gordon Swanson; **34(b)** Chris DeRidder and Hans VandenNieuwendijk; **35(b)** HUANG, CHI-FENG; **37(t)** Rena Schild; **37(b)** Israel Pabon; **38(b)** Fotosav; **39(tl)** Mikael Damkier; **39(b)** IM_photo; **40** Nodff; **41** Jiri Haureljuk; **42** StockphotoVideo; **43** Ersler Dmitry; **45** Jason L. Price; **46** Roberto Caucino; **48** Nioloxs; **49(a)** JJ pixs; **49(b)** Stormcab; **49(c)** Kameel4u; **49(d)** Lana K; **49(e)** Greenland; **51** Igor Stepovik; **53** DOPhoto; **54(tl)** SJ Travel Photo and Video; **54(tm)** Ieva Geneviciene; **54(tr)** Kiselev Andrey Valerevich; **54(bl)** Untitled; **54(bm)** Galyna Andrushko; **54(br)** Serp; **55** Ultimathule; **57(t)** PaSob; **57(b)** Elaine Barker; **60** Sue Stokes; **65** Sailorr; **68** Iness Arna; **71** VanderWolf Images; **72(m)** Altafulla; **73** Elena Elisseeva; **76(t)** Nikolae; **76(b)** Dgbomb; **77** Monkey Business Images; **78** Ene; **80** Andrey Arkusha; **81(l)** Miodrag Gajic; **81(r)** Dean Mitchell; **83** Thomas M Perkins; **84(tl)** VanderWolf Images; **84(bl)** TrotzOlga; **84(bm)** Asvolas; **84(tr)** Africa Studio; **84(br)** Yurlick; **85** TTL Media; **87** Karnizz; **90(tl)** Ian MacLellan; **90(bl)** Mikadun; **90(tr)** Aaron Amat; **90(br)** Mny-Jhee; **92(tl)** Flariviere; **92(tr)** Lebedeff; **92(bl)** Sergej Razvodovskij; **92(bm)** Margo Harrison; **93(l)** Dmitry_T; **93(r)** Skylines; **94(tl)** Mark Higgins; **94(bl)** Jaroslav Moravcik; **94(br)** Frederick R. Matzen; **98(tl)** Nate Allred; **98(tr)** Andrey Yurlov; **98(br)** Michaeljung; **99(tl)** Beerkoff; **99(tr)** Matka_Wariatka; **102(tl)** Greenland; **102(tr)** Andrei Zarubaika; **102(bl)** Phase4Studios; **102(br)** Uber Images; **104(tl)** Amanda Herron; **104(tm)** Kheng Guan Toh; **104(bl)** Grafnata; **104(bm)** Shamleen; **104(br)** Vladimir Mucibabic; **106(tl)** JeremyRichards; **106(bl)** Travelview; **108(tl)** JonMilnes; **108(tr)** ET1972; **108(bl)** Krzysztof Odziomek; **108(br)** Kromka; **110(tl)** Elena Moiseeva; **110(tr)** StockLite; **110(br)** Gravicapa; **111(tl)** Frances L Fruit; **111(tr)** Anneka; **111(bl)** Alsu; **111(br)** Orion-v; **112(tr)** Pavel L Photo and Video; **112(bl)** Carole Castelli; **112(br)** LIGHTWORK; **113** LuckyImages